The Story Teller
By
Alan Faraway

The Story Teller, is my sixth book of poems. Within these pages are stories, observations and fantasies. I love the imagination of children. Unlike us adults, they're not hampered by self-consciousness, they don't really care what people think of their stories and make believe worlds. We, as adults should encourage them, nurture their imaginations for they are the story tellers of the future. The film makers, the actors and the writers in the years ahead. This is why I have included a poem from an eight year old girl who sent one in to me, and for that I thank her and her parents. I hope you enjoy the contents of this offering and whatever you do in this life, I hope you find happiness, love and peace.

Many thanks

Alan Faraway

Alan Faraway

Other books by Alan Faraway

Pictures In My Head
Pagan Ways
Nature's Child
Reflections
Cherished Moments

Copyright © 2018 by A. Faraway and published by A. W. Smith. All rights reserved worldwide. No part of this publication may be replicated, redistributed, or given away in any form without the prior written consent of the author/ publisher or the terms relayed to you herein.

Contact Andrw4smith@sky.com

Contents

Title

A Note from Alan
(and the boring bit)
Contents
Angel of the night
Bring the magic back
Change
Cold, Cold Winter's Day
Coloured Lights
Compassion of Humanity
Destiny
Destiny Your Friend
Dog Walk
Don't laugh at me
Early morning sun
Farewell to a friend
For my father
Forest farewell
Gardeners
Getting old
Good drivers?
Happy New Year
How things might have been
I really love you so
I send my love
I write
Land of Nod
Last farewell
Leave no man behind
Legacy of mankind
Maybe

Meaning of Christmas?
My Oasis
My Pledge
When nature's cloak turns white
Never Again
Nostalgic Fashion
Not a tree hugger
Not my dream
October Night
One Chance
One Liners
One minute
Our first caravan trip
Pagan anniversary
Persephone
Plastic lives
Pussycats
Save for the rainy days
Shades of blue
Soldiers of the Queen
Soldier's Retreat
Some people
Special gift
Spirit of the night
Sweetly dream
Stonehenge
Take a look (around you)
Terror
The cold and icy sea*
The final question
The girl from across the pond
The good old days
The man beneath the tree
The story of Naradine

The story teller
They stood before the Colours
Times of me and you
When Nature's cloak turns white
When Santa Clause Got Stuck!
White witch of the woods
Acknowledgements

*By Evelyn Clifton-Bowley aged 8

Angel Of The Night

I was lost just like a child,
In a crowded market square,
Surrounded by misty faces,
Of people who didn't care,
They took me on a joy ride,
But the joy was just for them,
They took me for the fool I was,
When I really needed a friend.

Then I saw you smile at me,
And the smile was so sincere,
You touched my hand and suddenly,
The mist began to clear,
You whispered softly to me,
Told me all would be alright,
You came to me when I needed you,
Like an angel of the night.

And what of life before you came,
My dark and lonely years,
Those disastrous failed flirtations,
That could only end in tears,
The darkness that overcame me,
Closing out the light,
You know my deepest, darkest thoughts,
Like an angel of the night.

And when you kiss an angel,
The world's a better place,
The past is just a memory,
Another time in space,
Another chapter of your life,
That fades before the light,
And love becomes a halo,
Like the angel of the night.

I guess that once you've found love,
And you know that it's for real,
Then life again has a meaning,
The world has a different feel,
And when I look into your eyes,
They twinkle like soft starlight,
And I know that you'll forever be,
My angel of the night.

Bedtime Story

As it's almost time for bed,
I thought perhaps I might,
Tell you a bedtime story,
Before we say goodnight,
A tale of a friendly dragon,
And a little princess who,
Had golden hair entwined with stars,
And eyes of purest blue.

Put your head upon the pillow,
And I shall tuck you in,
Settle down and close your eyes,
And then I shall begin,
Put your teddy in beside you,
And cuddle him real tight,
And very soon you'll drift away,
With the spirit of the night.

Once, a long, long time ago,
In the land where dreams are made,
There lived a little princess,
Alina was her name,
She used to roam the orchards,
Within the castle grounds,
And listen to the songs of birds,
That sat upon the boughs.

Although she was a princess,
Alina was pretty sad,
She didn't have friends to play with,
Just a tortoise that she had,
But a tortoise is quite boring,
And it can't play hide and seek,
And It moves so very slowly,
Eating dandelion leaves.

From her window she saw the village children,
Playing in the street,
And watched them as they sat around,
On the village green to eat,
She'd sit and watch for hours,
And wished she could join in,
But her dad said that a princess,
Didn't do that sort of thing.

So Alina was very lonely,
And she'd wander off alone,
Through the halls and corridors,
Of her cold and empty home,
She'd go into the forest,
And there amongst the trees,
She'd watch the forest creatures,
As they foraged happily.

One day she went to the forest,
And the day was pretty hot,
She found her favourite clearing,
Which was her usual spot,
The trees had formed a circle,
And the grass was soft and clear,
The birds were singing in the trees,
Then the animals all came near.

She didn't know quite what to do,
They hadn't done this before,
The squirrels and the rabbits,
And even a wild boar,
All came up beside her,
But Alina wasn't scared,
She stroked the head of a soft skinned deer,
And cuddled a fluffy hare.

Then suddenly the sky went dark,
And she felt a rush of air,
She looked around and up and down,
And felt a little scared,
She heard the sound of wing beats,
Like the wings of a giant bird,
Then a dragon fell in front of her,
And rolled in the soft green earth.

Are you alright? Alina asked,
As it staggered to its feet,
The dragon shook its body and said,
Well that was pretty neat,
I usually topple forward,
And my nose goes in the dirt,
And I have to tell you little girl,
Sometimes that really hurts!

Then the dragon raised its scaly head,
And gave a fiery sneeze,
Which singed the tail of a squirrel,
That was sitting in the tree,
"Sorry" said the dragon,
In a kind of squirrelly voice,
As the squirrel patted down its tail,
And dropped a nut on Alina's tortoise.

Alina looked at the dragon,
As it stood upon the grass,
Its scales changed colour as it moved,
And then she said at last,
You don't seem very scary,
Not at all what I've been told,
In fact I think you're very nice,
And are you very old?

Well thank you said the dragon,
And in fact I'm still quite young,
I've lived almost a hundred years,
And had a lot of fun,
Now don't believe all that you hear,
All those tales you've been told,
Dragons are not that fearsome,
And knights are not that bold.

I haven't introduced myself,
How remiss of me he said,
I am known as Salim-Sar,
And he bowed his scaly head,
Pleased to meet you, the princess said,
I'm Alina, she replied,
And from that day Salim-Sar,
Was never far from her side.

They spent their days in the forest,
Saw many wonderful things,
And one day the dragon asked her,
Would you like to meet the fairy king?
Now you're making fun of me,
Alina said and picked her nails,
Everyone knows fairies only exist,
In those silly children's tales.

Oh pardon me said the dragon,
I forgot you know it all,
And then he sniffed at a hedgehog,
That turned into a ball,
Now don't start sulking Alina said,
As the dragon looked away,
I'm only saying what my father said,
Come on let's play a game.

Well your father doesn't know everything,
The dragon huffily replied,
The trouble is that folk like him,
Never use their eyes,
They only see what they want to see,
But there's so much more out there,
And to stifle your imagination,
Just really isn't fair.

I can show you a different world,
A world of magic and mystery.
A world so full of wonderful things,
If you put your trust in me,
You shouldn't spend your childhood years,
Alone and without much fun,
Not when there's so many things,
You can see when you are young.

Alina thought a little while,
At what the dragon said,
She looked around at the animals,
Who seemed to nod their heads,
Ok she said after quite some time,
But you have to promise me,
If you take me on a little trip,
I must be back in time for tea.

The dragon smiled and held out his paw,
Agreed he said and swished his tail,
Now climb upon my back princess,
And hold onto my scales,
And when Alina was ready,
He flapped his wings and up they flew,
Alina laughed at the startled hoot,
Of a sleepy eyed cuckoo.

High into the sky they went,
Through the candy floss of clouds,
Below they saw little figures walking,
Like ants upon the ground,
They flew toward a mountain,
And the dragon picked up speed,
They headed toward the mountain side,
And Alina let out a scream.

But they didn't crash into the jagged rocks,
As Alina thought they might,
But into a cave which she hadn't seen,
And out of the bright sunlight,
The darkness didn't last that long,
For the cave opened to reveal,
Purple grass and sparkling trees,
And twinkling daffodils.

They flew across this strange landscape,
In the lavender scented breeze,
And as they flew they saw below,
A swarm honey bees,
Their tiny wing beats made a tune,
That carried in the air,
The blossom trees held out their leaves,
And the bees just disappeared.

Below they saw a golden stream,
That flowed between purple hills,
And bright blue birds with silver wings,
Flew across a rainbow field,
They saw a town and castle,
With roads of purest white,
And a dome of coloured diamonds,
That sparkled in the light.

The dragon smiled and circled,
And landed in the castle grounds,
They were greeted by the king and queen,
And the crowd that gathered around,
It's good to see you Salim-Sar,
The king said with a smile,
We were wondering if you'd drop by,
For it has been quite a while.

Apologies your majesties,
I've been busy as you know,
I've brought a friend to see you,
From the land beyond the snow,
May I present Alina,
Then crouched so the king could see,
Pleased to meet you the queen then said,
And may I say you're so pretty.

Why thank you said Alina,
I'm pleased to meet you too,
Salim-Sar has told me many tales,
And now I see they're true,
Come with me the queen then said,
Let me show you around,
And then we'll have some tea and cakes,
Out here in the castle grounds.

So off they went together,
Alina and the queen,
No one back home would ever believe,
The things that she would see,
The diamond flower garden,
A golden fountain in the hall,
And the moving pictures that spoke to her,
From their frames upon the wall.

She saw a herd of unicorns,
That vanished then reappeared,
And on the edge of the twinkling woods,
A herd of snow white deer,
A stag and hind were leading,
Their antlers were silver and gold,
And the queen said they were the parents,
And their young were not that old.

They walked around the castle grounds,
And out onto the moors,
Then through a little village,
With brightly coloured doors,
Alina bent down to smell a rose,
Of purple, blue and red,
But the rose disappeared into the ground,
You scared it the queen smiled and said.

They went back to the courtyard,
Where a feast had been prepared,
There were drinks and wonderful little treats,
And people had gathered there,
Salim-Sar and the king were talking,
As the children all played games,
Alina and the queen joined in,
And they made up silly names.

Then came the time to leave them,
Salim-Sar bade them farewell,
The queen told Alina she must return,
To see the mirror caves and wells,
Alina promised that she would,
And thanked them for the day,
But the queen could see in Alina's eyes,
She was sad to go away.

Come on Alina the dragon said,
It's time I took you home,
The king gave Alina a talisman,
Now you'll never be alone,
Always keep this with you,
We're only a wish away,
Think of us and you will find,
You can come back by night or day.

Alina thanked the king and queen,
For their hospitality,
Then climbed onto the dragons back,
And waved farewell quite cheerily,
Thank you Salim-Sar she said,
As they flew into the sky,
That was the very best of days,
And a tear formed in her eyes.

She heard a voice gently say to her,
Wake up you sleepy head,
She stirred and opened her bright blue eyes,
Where's Salim-Sar she said,
Who's Salim-Sar her mother asked,
You've been sleeping for a while,
Come on my love it's breakfast time,
Her mother said with a smile.

She told her mother about Salim-Sar,
And the fairy King and Queen,
She told her of the magical land,
And all that she had seen,
Her mother listened and smiled,
That was a wonderful dream she said,
But dragons and fairy kings and queens,
Only live inside your head.

The years they passed so quickly,
Into a woman Alina grew,
She always felt a presence near,
But what it was, she never knew,
She often thought of Salim-Sar
And the wonderful times they shared,
They were not dreams like her mother said,
They were real so she didn't care.

One day her father introduced her to,
A prince from a far off land,
He was quite tall and handsome,
And he looked so very grand,
You two will marry her father said,
And our lands will then be one,
Don't argue with me it's all arranged,
The deal it has been done!

Alina didn't want to marry,
But it seemed she had no choice,
The prince was a very boring man,
And she couldn't stand his squeaky voice!
The wedding day began to loom,
Preparations were all in hand,
And Alina thought of Salim-Sar,
The fairy queen and that magical land.

She began to sort her wardrobe out,
And the boxes of her childhood things,
A couple of dolls and a hairbrush,
Her make up mirror and a couple of rings,
She looked through the pocket of a forgotten coat,
When something touched her hand,
She pulled it out and to her surprise,
She had found the lost talisman!

She recalled what the fairy king had said,
So many years ago,
We are just a wish away,
And she wondered if that were so,
So she held the talisman very tight,
And wished with all her heart,
Then suddenly Salim-Sar appeared,
Which gave her quite a start.

Well about time too! He smiled and said,
It's been so many years,
Alina tried to hug his neck,
Salim-Sar!, she cried through the tears,
Now don't go on, Salim-Sar told her,
All will be alright,
Did you really think I'd leave you here,
To face this terrible plight?

I've been watching you throughout the years,
And I've seen the good you've done,
Your heart is true and compassionate,
And this prince is not the one,
Your father's wrong to force this on you,
He's doing it for his selfish greed,
He wants more power and more land too,
He doesn't care what his daughter needs.

I want to go away from here,
Alina sobbed and cried,
I really don't want to marry this man,
And the tears flowed from her eyes,
Nor shall you Salim-Sar whispered,
His voice so gentle and soft,
Climb upon my back my dear,
And then we shall be off.

Just then the prince with guards rushed in,
They'd heard Alina cry out,
Salim-Sar looked at them,
And Alina was in no doubt,
They'd kill her wonderful Salim-Sar,
They were ready to attack,
Go away! She screamed at them,
Then climbed upon his back.

Kill the beast! The prince called out,
And drew his shiny sword,
Salim-Sar said to Alina,
We'll be fine, you have my word,
The soldiers lunged toward him,
But their swords broke on his scales,
Salim-Sar began to smile and said,
I'll squash you like tiny snails.

Don't hurt them please Salim-Sar she begged,
Salim-Sar just smiled and winked,
Then flicked his tongue and the handsome prince,
Knocked over Alina's drink,
The liquid in the mug was hot,
And it spilled into his shoe,
Alina laughed as he hopped about,
His squeaky voice shouting ooh, ooh, ooh!

Salim-Sar breathed out a little flame,
And the soldiers turned to run,
Pushing each other to get out the door,
And patting down their burning bums,
The only person left in the room,
Was the prince with his soaking shoe,
Alina looked at the whimpering prince,
And said there's something I must tell you.

The prince looked up at Alina,
As she sat on the dragons back,
I don't want to marry you she said,
The prince looked relieved at that,
And I don't want to marry you,
The prince readily replied,
For I'm in love with another,
And she shall be my bride.

Our fathers both insisted,
That our union should take place,
They had no thought for what we want,
They should've asked in any case,
They want this wedding for their own greed,
So I guess it serves them right,
I hope you find true happiness,
And you have a wonderful life.

Sorry about your foot she said,
I hope it's not too bad,
And I hope you have a good life too,
May your days be joyful not sad,
Sorry to interrupt you both,
Salim-Sar said with a cough,
But I really think that we should go,
This farewell is quite enough.

Goodbye young prince Alina said,
As the dragon beat its wings,
It's tail caught on the curtains,
And pulled them off their rings,
The king came into the room to see,
His daughter fly into the sky,
Sat astride the dragons back,
And a tear formed in his eyes.

It's all your fault the queen told him,
You never really understood,
And you never listened to a word she said,
Like I've often said you should,
All she wanted was your love,
Now you've driven her away,
I said your greed would cause you pain,
Now the time has come to pay.

Soon Salim-Sar and Alina,
Were in the land of the fairy king,
There the queen gave Alina,
A very special ring,
She said always keep this with you,
And your beauty will never fade,
As long as you don't leave the Kingdom,
For more than five whole days.

The fairy queen said to Alina,
Let me tell you about Salim-Sar,
He's a magic dragon,
And he'll always be in your heart,
He'll always be there when you need him,
And he'll always be by your side,
He'll protect you with all the power he has,
Every day for the rest of your life.

So Alina lived in the castle,
With the fairy king and queen,
She fell in love with a handsome man,
A perfect end to a perfect dream,
She lived so very happily,
In a house in the castle grounds,
And Salim-Sar with the king and queen,
Would often come around.

As for the prince with the squeaky voice,
He married the one he loved,
They lived in a castle far away,
Kept horses, deer and doves,
Alina's father became a better king,
He listened to what people said,
Upon his castle turret flew,
A flag with a dragons head.

Alina would visit her mum and dad,
Helped by the fairy king and queen,
And she'd tell them of the life she had,
And the things that she has seen,
They listened quite intently,
As her children played in the hall,
And Salim-Sar played with them,
So everyone lived happily after all.

Bring the magic back

We just don't seem to talk   anymore,
We never have much to say,
And so we live the same routine,
Each minute of every day,
We seem to have lost the sparkle,
Somewhere down the track,
And I wish that we could find a way,
To bring the magic back.

When we first set out on this road,
We had such fun filled times,
We made our plans and set our dreams,
And said that we'd be fine,
We used to talk for hours,
And laugh at daft wise cracks,
And I wish that we could find a way,
To bring that magic back.

Because now we sit in silence,
Staring at the TV screen,
Rejecting our reality,
For someone else's dream,
Lost in a world of fantasy,
Of fiction mixed with fact,
And I wish that we could find a way,
To bring the magic back.

The wonderful love that we both share,
Will never fade away,
The tenderness of your embrace,
Still thrills me day by day,
But I wish we could find the sparkle,
That somehow we now lack,
How I wish that we could find a way,
To bring the magic back.

So let's escape this rat race,
Let's go out for the day,
Let's go down to the river bank,
And watch time slip away,
Let's do something crazy,
Throw caution in a sack,
And let us search to find a way,
To bring the magic back.

We're too young to drop the portcullis,
Raise the drawbridge and grow old,
We should open up the windows,
Let sunlight replace the cold,
We should return to yesterday,
Now what do you say to that?
And together my love we'll find a way,
To bring the magic back.

Change

If you could live your life again,
What changes would you make,
Would you make the same decisions,
And make the same mistakes?
Or would you do things differently,
Would you choose another way,
Even though you wouldn't be,
The person you are today.

For history defines us,
It makes us who we are,
Our past gives us our future,
The experiences and scars,
And if you changed your history,
Just one thing would be enough,
To alter your whole future,
But would you be with the one you love.

I'll leave you with that question,
Something to think about,
Maybe you would change your life,
Perhaps you'd have no doubt,
Or maybe if you thought a while,
You wouldn't change a thing,
For who knows what the future holds,
Or what a change may bring.

Cold, Cold Winters Day

Snowflakes, like confetti,
Falling softly to the ground,
Children making snowmen,
Some too thin and some too round,
Shrieks of laughter as they slide,
On dodgy homemade sleighs,
Down a snowy hillside,
On a cold, cold winters day.

Old folk treading gingerly,
On pavements white with snow,
Remember times when they were young,
So very long ago,
When they skidded down the hillside,
In the sledges they had made,
Laughing, playing, having fun,
On a cold, cold winters day.

Stranded on the highways,
As the snow falls thick and fast,
They'll be there for hours,
Freezing in their cars,
Vehicles left abandoned,
And that is where they'll stay,
Until someone comes to rescue them,
On this cold, cold winters day.

The homeless look for shelter,
And somewhere warm to hide,
Not everyone has the luxury,
Of a welcome fireside,
An Eastern wind is blowing,
Bringing misery this way,
As we brace ourselves for icy blasts,
And a cold, cold winters day.

Boiler breakdown in the home,
Central heating up the creek,
The freezing cold will take the lives,
Of the very old and weak,
Emergency services on full alert,
As more snow heads our way,
There'll be disruption and more chaos,
On this cold, cold winters day.

Trains brought to a standstill,
And the snow keeps coming down,
Panic buying at the shops,
Amid nature's winter gown,
Vehicles sliding here and there,
Carnage on the carriageways,
And I wonder at the human cost,
On this cold, cold winters day.

But the snowflakes, like confetti,
Form a carpet on the ground,
Icy winds that blow so hard,
Turns it into drifts and mounds,
But the children shriek with laughter,
As they slide on homemade sleighs,
Down the snowy hillsides,
On a cold, cold winters day.

Coloured Lights

Coloured lights and tinsel,
Gifts beneath the tree,
Eyes that view the packages,
And Wonder excitedly,
What hides beneath the wrapping,
What treasures do they hold,
Soon there will be smiles,
From the young ones and the old.

Coloured lights and tinsel,
Singers at the door,
Warm mulled wine and hot mince pies,
Who could ask for more,
Families all will gather,
Full of festive cheer,
What a glorious wonderful way,
To celebrate the year.

Coloured lights and tinsel,
Candy cane and little bells,
Children grow to adulthood,
And maybe they will tell,
The little children of their own,
Of a wonderful Christmas night,
When coloured lights and tinsel,
Brought them such delight.

Compassion of Humanity

I huddle in a doorway,
So cold and so alone,
I do not have the luxury,
Of a warm enticing home,
On the streets is where I live,
Where I struggle to survive,
Each day I watch humanity,
Go about their daily lives.

I'm a faceless individual,
A shadow no one sees,
A castaway, a non de script,
Rejected by society,
I'm easily forgotten,
Like a dream of yesterday,
People may well glance at me,
But quickly look away.

I've sold my pride and dignity,
And begged to passer's by,
In the hope to raise some money,
To keep the hunger satisfied,
But I'm turned away from warm cafés,
Because they say I stink,
But all I want is a hearty meal,
And something hot to drink.

Each day and night I run the risk,
Of being beaten and abused,
No one ever steals from me,
For I have nothing else to lose,
Except a sleeping bag full of holes,
And the clothes upon my back,
And boots that let the water in,
And an old threadbare rucksack.

So I seek the quiet alleyways,
To become invisible,
Sleeping in the shadows,
Where I hope I'm not revealed,
And when I wake I'll sell my pride,
Hope someone pity's me,
For hunger is my only friend,
And my only company.

There are others just like me,
Hungry, alone and cold,
And each has a different story,
That will never ever be told,
For no one wants to listen,
No one wants to hear,
They don't want to think that we exist,
But we do and we live in fear.

So we huddle in the doorways,
So cold and so alone,
We do not have the luxury,
Of a warm enticing home,
On the streets is where we live,
Where we struggle to survive,
And the compassion of humanity,
Blindly pass us by.

Destiny

The road of life is a mystery,
A perpetual blind bend,
We don't know where it leads us,
We only know, one day, it ends
So as we walk this rocky road,
This twisting, untrodden track,
We put our faith in destiny,
And keep the demon off our back.

So will you be rich and famous,
Or a villain on the run,
Will you be the peacemaker,
Or the one who holds the gun,
Will you be a captain of industry,
Or will you struggle to survive,
No one knows what lies ahead,
Destiny will decide.

We may try to take a different road,
As we travel along the track,
But if it doesn't lead where we should go,
Then destiny will bring us back,
Back to the path we've been chosen for,
Back to our own special road,
To fulfil what destiny has for us,
As surely as the cockerel crows.

Whatever road is mapped for you,
That's the path you'll tread,
So take the hand of destiny,
And allow yourself to be led,
When you reach your destination,
And at last you are set free,
Fear not the final curtain,
For you've fulfilled your destiny.

Destiny Your Friend

Life is clouded in mystery,
You may look but will not see,
What lies ahead, along the path,
You'll only see what's in the past.

You will not feel the wind of change,
Or see it silently rearrange,
The world that you had come to know,
Through the rain and sun or winters snow.

You cannot change your road you see,
For what's set out is what will be,
So embrace the life you have today,
For tomorrow will soon be yesterday.

Joy may pass and tears may flow,
But in your heart you'll always know,
That I will love you until the end,
For I'm your destiny,
I am your friend.

Dog Walk

I took our dogs for a morning walk,
On the hills of the Sussex Downs,
Charlie our little Jack Russel,
And Rosie our black Greyhound,
The sun was in its duvet,
And the moon was playing a game,
Of peekaboo between the clouds,
And the stars were doing the same.

It was a cold and frosty morning,
When we left our nice warm home,
The neighbours I thought we're still in bed,
As we walked through the streets alone,
The ice was hoping to catch a lift,
For it clung to car windscreens,
Where unseen fingers drew patterns,
To say Jack Frost had been.

Rosie was wearing her padded coat,
Well a greyhound's skin is thin,
Charlie's fur is very thick,
And the cold doesn't bother him,
I was in my big warm coat,
With a fleecy hat on my head,
And as they sniffed I thought to myself,
Perhaps I should've stayed in bed!

It wasn't long before we reached,
The entrance to the park,
And as we entered I heard the cows,
Lowing somewhere in the dark,
I wondered why they weren't inside,
Away from the winter chill,
And I bet the farmer didn't spend the night,
On that cold and icy hill.

I let the dogs free from their leads,
And threw a bright glow ball,
Charlie darted after it,
But no interest from Rosie at all,
She was content to sniff the ground,
As we wandered toward the hill,
In the darkness of the morning,
While the park was quiet and still.

We'd been out about an hour,
When the sun decided to rise,
And resume its favourite pastime,
Of chasing the moon across the sky.
The frosty leaves were glistening,
In the first rays of the sun,
And it must've woken Rosie up,
For she took of on a looping run.

I wandered across the hilltop,
Throwing the ball and looking around,
Charlie chasing after it,
And Rosie still sniffing the ground,
Then suddenly her ears pricked up,
She stood there perfectly still,
Like a guardsman standing at Buck House*,
A statue in the winter chill.

Her eyes transfixed on a clump of gorse,
About forty yards away,
Something had clearly caught her eye,
But what it was I couldn't say,
Then a rabbit broke its cover,
And made a dash for home,
Scurrying across the open ground,
And into the danger zone.

Rosie took off like a rocket,
Like an Exocet in pursuit,
Running down the furry beast,
And there was nothing I could do,
The hunted and the hunter,
No rifles, traps or snares,
Nature would decide today,
If a life would be ended here.

She didn't need to hunt for food,
But her instincts had kicked in,
The rabbit dodged and weaved and ran,
And the pursuer was fast gaining,
The gap between them was closing,
She ignored my calls to heel,
I put myself in the rabbits place,
And I wondered how I would feel.

Just a couple of strides to go,
And the jaws of death would close,
Suddenly the rabbit disappeared,
He'd managed to get back home,
I think he made it just in time,
For Rosie's head was bent,
This time the rabbit was lucky,
For it was almost heaven sent.

I imagined the little rabbit,
Sitting with its family,
Telling them of his exploits,
And sharing a pot of tea,
Telling them of the dangers,
Out there in the danger zone,
And how he'd outran a greyhound,
To barely make it home.

Rosie was disappointed,
She sniffed at the rabbit hole,
Hoping it would come back out,
And she could have another go,
Finally she left it,
And wandered back to me,
We carried on then with our walk,
And Charlie chased the ball happily.

Her disappointment soon forgotten,
She wandered off and sniffed a bush,
Charlie barked at a flock of birds,
And growled at a passing rook,
Then we turned and headed home,
Along a frozen track,
I, for one, would be so glad,
When we finally got back.

We left the hills and crossed the park,
And the neighbours had woken up,
More people now upon the streets,
As homeward bound we trudged,
The icy wind had risen,
And now was blowing hard,
Rosie sniffed and Charlie barked,
And saw off a noisy car.

We got back home and opened the door,
Our walk now at an end,
The dogs made a beeline for their food,
And the warmth hugged me like a friend,
A milky coffee was waiting,
And I clasped it with cold hands,
And I hoped the weather would be fine,
When I'd take them out again.

Anyone who has a dog,
I'm sure will understand,
That they are like our children,
And we do the best we can,
We love them and we care for them,
Although they're pests sometimes,
But they're loyal and they're loving,
And I'm really glad they're mine.

*Buck House: Slang term for Buckingham Palace

Don't Laugh At Me

Don't laugh at me 'cos I'm different,
Don't think that I'm a fool,
Don't look at me in horror,
For I am human just like you,
Maybe it's hard for me to speak,
And maybe my limbs don't work,
But I feel pain and I can cry,
When you whisper, point and smirk,

Don't laugh at me 'cos I'm different,
Don't mock my disabilities,
For I am not a sideshow freak,
And you really don't know me,
Perhaps I can't do the things you do,
And I won't win no beauty shows,
But my heart has more compassion,
Than you will ever know.

So don't laugh at me 'cos I'm different,
Understanding is the key,
But go ahead and live your life,
Be thankful you are free,
Free from a dysfunctional body,
And people who don't understand,
Free from the whispers and sideways looks,
And the ignorance of man.

Early Morning Spring

Walking in the countryside,
Blossoms on the trees,
The scent of wild flowers,
Drifting gently on the breeze,
The early dew like diamonds,
Hang on cobwebs in mid air,
In the early morning spring you'll hear,
Sweet birdsong everywhere.

The cunning fox is foraging,
And the deer graze happily,
Nature at its very best,
A wonderful sight to see,
The sun on the far horizon,
Makes its way into the sky,
In the early morning spring you'll see,
True magic before your eyes.

So far away from the city noise,
So far away from the sounds,
Away from the polluted atmosphere,
That rises from the ground,
Away from overcrowded streets,
Where no one seems to care,
In the early morning spring you'll feel,
The beauty of clean air.

But how long before the countryside,
Becomes a sprawling town,
How long before those mighty trees,
Come crashing to the ground,
How long before those ancient paths,
Become smelling littered streets,
In the early morning spring no more,
Will wildlife roam and eat.

I hope it never comes to this,
I really hope it don't,
I hope we learn before it's too late,
But of course I know we won't,
Because we are too short sighted,
We live for the here and now,
In the early morning spring we'll find,
No answer to the question "How?

So take a walk in the countryside,
See the blossoms on the trees,
Smell the scent of wild flowers,
Drifting gently on the breeze,
See the early dew like diamonds,
Hang on cobwebs in mid air,
For in the early morning spring, one day,
This beauty may not be there.

Farewell To A Friend

Farewell to you,
My dear faithful friend,
Our journey together,
Has come to an end,
Though your spirit has left me,
To dwell somewhere new,
Each morning I wake,
I know I'll see you.

Farewell to you friend,
I'll remember and smile,
The times that we had,
When we walked for miles,
Across open fields,
And valleys and hills,
Passed rivers and streams,
And wild daffodils.

Farewell my old friend,
Till we meet again,
And together we'll walk,
On that spiritual plain,
Though just a dog,
You were true to the end,
Never forgotten,
Goodbye my old friend.

For My Father

These words are for my father,
With thanks for the times we had,
The things that he passed onto me,
And his comfort when I was sad,
The evenings we spent watching sunsets,
As we questioned the world, him and me,
When we sat and talked for hours,
And we rarely disagreed.

I was only a child then,
I asked what a child might ask,
And he answered in words that I understood,
It was a pleasure for him, not a task,
And we'd sit in the long summer evenings,
To watch the sun slip away from the sky,
And I'd go to bed quite contented,
Knowing he'd always be at my side.

Then as the years slipped past us,
I spent hours on my own,
Not wanting the help of my father,
Believing that I was full grown,
I'd watch him through my window,
As he gazed at the setting sun,
And I'd get ready to hit the town,
I was young and craving fun.

So no longer did I sit with him,
And question the world we saw,
I stayed out late almost every night,
Sometimes not returning till dawn,
I didn't sit with him to watch sunsets,
For I had my own life to lead,
And our conversations seemed pointless,
Because rarely did we agree.

But he was always there to offer advice,
Whenever things went wrong,
His words were kind and gentle,
His loving arms felt strong,
He never seemed to judge me,
Though I'm sure I drove him mad,
And when I finally flew the nest,
He smiled though I knew he was sad.

The sand in the hour glass kept falling,
And so, a few decades on,
I sat again with my father,
And watched the dying sun,
As it slipped beyond the horizon,
We'd talk of things endlessly,
And we questioned the world together,
And we seldom disagreed.

But the world keeps on revolving,
And time, on life, takes its toll,
People pass on to another world,
Whether they're very young or old,
Now I sit alone in my garden,
And think of the times gone by,
With my father, in spirit, beside me,
I watch as the sun leaves the sky.

Forest Farewell

I said goodbye to the forest,
Farewell to the trees and birds,
Goodbye to the leaves of autumn,
Now a carpet on the earth,
Farewell to the marshes and bracken,
Goodbye to the silver streams,
Now I'll walk those ancient byways,
But only in my dreams.

I said goodbye to the sunlight,
That filtered through the trees,
Farewell to the deer and squirrels,
And the gentle soft warm breeze,
Goodbye to the woodland creatures,
The sweet sound of birdsong,
Farewell to the open wilderness,
Where William once did roam.

For I must return to the city,
To the chaos and the noise,
Back to the daily grind of work,
No more to roam the moors,
I return to civilisation,
If that is what it is,
But my heart remains in the forest,
And the caress of nature's kiss.

So farewell to the open meadows,
One day I shall return,
Once more to walk your ancient tracks,
Through your mighty oaks and ferns,
To sit beside your silver streams,
At one in nature's arms,
Farewell, you ancient woodland,
To your beauty and your charm.

Gardeners

You and I are gardeners,
We'll watch our flower grow,
We'll keep it safe,
This precious thing,
This seed that we have sewn,
This delicate, fragile, tender thing,
We'll nurture and watch it bloom,
Dancing in the summer sun,
Slumbering beneath the moon.

You and I are gardeners,
We'll make our flower strong,
We'll feed it well,
We'll keep it warm,
Keep it where it should belong,
Throughout its life we'll do our best,
Though the years will pass too soon,
And one day we'll have memories,
Of our flower now in full bloom.

You and I are gardeners,
Other flowers we may raise,
We'll treat them all with tender love,
As they grow throughout the days,
And in the twilight of our years,
When our flowers are fully grown,
We'll know we've raised good gardeners,
With little flowers of their own.

Getting Old

My hair is fast receding,
What's left has now turned grey,
And the creases on my face has shown,
That time has passed my way,
The hair gel and the stylists,
I just don't need them now,
And the anti-ageing wrinkle cream,
Never worked anyhow.

My brain tells me I'm twenty,
My body says it's a lie,
I can't do the things I used to do,
Although I really try,
I look at all the youngsters,
As I shuffle here and there,
I'd like to run a marathon,
But I can barely make the stairs!

The days of chasing pretty girls,
And partying all night long,
And staying up to greet the sun,
Alas, those days are gone,
Now it's a milky drink at nine o'clock,
And off to bed for me,
I'll snuggle beneath my duvet,
And I hope to sleep soundly.

Tomorrow I'll shuffle up to the shop,
It'll take an age I know,
And I'm pretty sure that in the night,
That hill I climb must grow,
I'll be wheezing like a steam train,
When at last I reach the top,
And I guess that on the way, at least,
A dozen times I'll stop.

It's no fun getting old you know,
But that's what you will do,
So don't laugh at me when I shuffle past,
One day this will be you,
So live your life of merriment,
Remember youth's a flame we burn,
And one day in the future,
What you've borrowed must be returned.

I hope to make it till morning,
And see the sun rise one more time,
I'll potter about in my lonely world,
And bring my youth to mind,
Maybe I will see you,
In the early morning light,
But now it's time I was in bed,
So at least for now…….good night.

Good Drivers?

We see them on the motorways,
In the cities and the towns,
Those lunatics behind the wheel,
Driving just like clowns,
Weaving in and out of traffic,
Undertaking without a care,
Just so they can get in front,
In their rush to get nowhere.

They've got one hand on the steering wheel,
The other on the phone,
They'll rev their engines at traffic lights,
Thinking they're at Silverstone,
They'll leave the lights at breakneck speed,
Not thinking of the consequence,
And when they have an accident,
They'll protest their innocence.

They've watched those Fast and Furious films,
Or they think they're at Brands Hatch,
But the driving skills they think they have,
Is something they sadly lack,
They'll tell you they're good drivers,
And overtake on those blind bends,
But don't they know the cemetery's full,
Of good drivers just like them!

Traffic cones and marker posts,
To them they don't mean a thing,
They'll wait until they have no choice,
Before forcing their way in,
Because for them rules don't apply,
And you're only in their way,
And if you don't give way to them,
You're going have a real bad day!

There's never any police around,
When these fools are on the road,
Jumping lights 'cos they can't wait,
And they're in X Box mode,
They think they're playing Mario Cart,
They really must get ahead,
But it's usually the innocent,
That tends to wind up dead.

If only these people realised,
They're playing with other's lives,
And that their haste will only save,
About thirty seconds of time,
Vehicles are quite expensive,
But a life is worth much more,
Maybe they'll only understand,
When they hear the clang of a prison door.

Happy New Year

Step into a brand new year,
Let the old year fade away,
Look toward the future,
In the hope of better days.
I wish you all the happiness,
May your wishes and your dreams,
Be everything you hope they would,
No regrets of what might have been.

Step into a brand new year,
As the door closes on the past,
May you find what you are searching for,
In the sand of life's hour glass,
May the sun above you always shine,
May your path through life be clear,
And most of all I wish for you,
The happiest of New Year's.

How Things Might Have Been

Paint for me a picture,
Sing to me a song,
Write for me a true romance,
That lasts a whole life long,
Give me hope and happiness,
Wrapped inside a dream,
And placed within a little box,
Of how things might have been.

Bring to me a ring of stars,
In the sea of floating hearts,
Bring to me a fantasy,
Of love made in the dark,
Show me true devotion,
That no one's ever seen,
All tucked inside a little box,
Marked how things might have been.

But you won't paint a picture,
Or sing to me your song,
You won't give me a ring of stars,
To build my life upon,
So I'll flounder in the sea of hearts,
With my fantasies and dreams,
And my little box of trinkets,
Of how things might have been.

I Really Love You So

There's only one thing that I want,
One thing that I desire,
One thing that turns these sleeping embers,
Into a raging fire,
The only thing that sets my heartbeat,
Racing through the roof,
And that's love I always see,
Whenever I look at you.

You make me feel like a sun kissed beach,
Refreshed like a mountain stream,
You make me feel like a wispy cloud,
In a beautiful summers dream,
You set my pulses dancing,
And somewhere deep inside,
I feel the tingly, tiny wings,
Of a million butterflies.

So tell me that you love me,
And that your love is true,
Tell me that in all the world,
I'm the only one for you,
Then hold me tight and kiss me,
And never let me go,
Because you're the only one for me,
And I really love you so.

I Send My Love

For so many years I lived without love,
My world was dark and grey,
The sun never shone but rain always fell,
Each minute of every day,
I was all alone in a strange dark world,
Where time slipped by so fast,
Each second an hour, each hour a year,
And dreams were ghosts of the past.

Then a shaft of light pierced the gloomy sky,
A beacon of hope shone bright,
And the darkness faded as a brand new dawn,
Stripped away the black cloak of night,
I felt the sun and the wind upon my face,
I felt alive once more,
You set me free from that strange dark world,
Your love was the key to the door.

Now my imagination rises,
From the confines of my head,
My thoughts escape and disappear,
Somewhere overhead,
Some of them I recapture,
But they just don't seem the same,
For they return a jumbled mess,
Mutilated, rearranged.

So I put my pen to paper,
And hurriedly I write,
Before my thoughts and ideas escape,
To disappear in flight,
And somewhere in the tangled mess,
Of the words upon the page,
Are my feelings and my love for you,
And they will never be backstage.

I know I ramble on sometimes,
And I don't always get things right,
But this little heart of mine,
Beats with sheer delight,
Because my days are so much brighter,
Just knowing you are here,
You are the best thing in my life,
And I always want you near.

So my love I write these words,
To send them home to you,
And I hope that you can understand,
Why I love you as I do,
I hope that when you read this,
Then you will comprehend,
Why I do the things I do,
And why I'll love you until the end.

I Write

I write for the sad and lonely,
Whose lives are in despair,
I write for those who turn for help,
But find there's no-one there,
And I write for all the children,
Whose lives are torn apart,
By callous uncaring zealots,
Who really have no heart.

I write for the many people,
Whose lives are made a hell,
From the bigoted, narrow minded fools,
Who will never see so well,
And I write for those that suffer,
Whose lives are steeped in fear,
Who's silent screams and muffled yells,
Fall upon deaf ears.

I write for the young and old folk,
For the homeless on the streets,
I write for those that have no voice,
In this world so full of grief,
And I write for those who have a dream,
That never will come true,
I write for those that search for love,
And I write for folk like you.

I write in the hope the human race,
Will one day realise,
That through its destructive selfishness,
This world will surely die,
And if one day the world awakes,
To find there is no pain,
Then perhaps the words I've written,
Will not have been in vain.

Insane Maybe

My temple is my garden,
The hills and fields so wild,
I pray to the God and Goddess
So says the pagan child,
I live in peace and harmony,
With nature I am one,
I follow the ancient teachings,
And I bring harm to none.

My church is made of mortar and brick,
I pray to God on high,
I sing to Him my praises,
So says the Christian child,
I live in peace and harmony,
The Good Book is my guide,
I pray that there is peace on earth,
Beneath God's watchful eye.

My temple is the holy mosque,
And Allah is by my side,
The Imam leads us all in prayer,
So says the Muslim child,
I pray that there is worldwide peace,
And all can live as one,
Each and every one of us,
That lives beneath His sun.

The people of this fragile world,
Want peace and harmony,
All religions want that too,
So to me it's a mystery,
Why we have to fight and kill,
And say it's in God's name,
Maybe we don't want peace at all,
Because perhaps we're all insane.

Land of Nod

Life is clouded in mystery,
We cannot see what the future is,
We can't see the many turns and twists,
Or when comes that final kiss,
But is it really all that bad,
Not knowing what the future holds,
For if we did would our lives be sad,
More bitter, uncaring and cold.

And shall we forever wander,
Across the rocky land of Nod,
Caste out from the garden of Eden,
To search in vain for God.
And if by chance we found Him,
I wonder what we'd say,
Would He grant to us salvation,
Or shake his head and walk away.

For are we not destroying,
The very thing that He gave us,
This oasis in the galaxy,
We're slowly turning into dust,
Releasing poisons into the air,
Killing all that's in our way,
Becoming more cold and heartless,
Each minute of every day.

Death is the equaliser,
It'll come to you and me,
Rich or poor we're all the same,
When we join that company,
So maybe it's good we cannot see,
What the future has in store,
So we can live in ignorance,
And always strive for more.

Perhaps that's why we wander,
In this forsaken land of Nod,
In this world just East of Eden,
In our fruitless search for God,
If we found find Him, would we ask Him,
And would He tell us why,
Why He created this beautiful Earth,
Just to watch it die.

Last Farewell

The ink stains on the paper,
Reveal my last farewell,
For my time to leave the human race has come.
Although you'll see my body,
It's just an empty shell,
My spirit and my soul has now moved on.

Moved on to another dimension,
A different place and time,
So, you see, I haven't really died,
I've set out on a journey,
And you know that I'll be fine,
When I walk with friends across the bridge of sighs.

It's a journey we all undertake,
When our time on earth is done,
And you know that we'll be gone for quite a while,
But we won't make this trip alone,
For other souls will come,
And the ferryman will greet us with a smile.

I hope that when you think of me,
There'll be a smile behind your eyes,
As you recall those silly things that I once did,
Remember me with kindness,
And laugh at the things I tried
The adult that would sometimes become a kid.

I'm sorry I've had to leave you,
It's hard to understand,
That now I'm just a memory of your past,
But I hope the moments that we had,
Those precious times we shared,
Will stay forever deep within your heart.

So live a long and happy life,
Make every moment count,
Until it's time to make your way to the summer land,
For when your time on earth is through
You'll leave sweet memories,
And the ferryman will be your guiding hand.

So paint a smile and do not cry,
Be glad for all we had,
Maybe we'll meet in the future, who can tell,
And perhaps we'll have adventures,
Soulmates once again,
But for now I leave you with my last farewell.

Leave No Man Behind

From the streets of Northern Ireland,
To the deserts of Iraq,
From the icy hills of the Falkland Isles,
To Afghanistan's dusty tracks,
The British soldier faced his foe,
Put his life upon the line,
And the silent motto of the brothers in arms,
Is to leave no man behind.

As a fresh faced youth he volunteered,
To serve the country of his birth,
To protect the weak and innocent,
To help make a safer world,
He had the guts to stand and fight,
Now the horrors invade his mind,
He served the country that he loves,
And he left no man behind.

He did his country's bidding,
By air and land and sea,
Brothers and sisters arm in arm,
On the streets of a strange country,
The bombs and bullets took its toll,
On their bodies and their minds,
But in their darkest hours,
They left no man behind.

Now they've returned to civilian life,
Isolated in a strange new world,
Some carry injuries that are plain to see,
Others have tormented souls,
Civilians can never understand,
They're ignorant, uncaring, unkind,
But the serviceman is never alone,
For no man is left behind.

The demons come to haunt me,
At night when it's dark and still,
I hear the screams of the dying,
See the limbless on the hill,
Together we carry our comrades,
Back home behind the lines,
Together we mourn for the ones we lost,
But we left no man behind.

Survivor's guilt and anger,
Leads to whisky, beer and wine,
Relationships are hard to maintain,
And it don't get better with time,
But we find a way to deal with it,
And help is there to find,
And the memory that echoes in the brain,
Is leave no man behind.

Our duty may be over,
But the scars will never heal,
P.T.S.D the enemy now,
And that's very hard to kill,
Those that served have a story,
That may come in the fullness of time,
But regardless of the danger,
We left no man behind.

Legacy Of Mankind

They were born beneath a blazing sun,
They were born so wild and free,
They grew so very big and strong,
With tusks of Ivory,
Then man the destroyer came along,
He came and killed them all,
Now all that's left of these wonderful beasts,
Are ivory trinkets upon man's wall.

They were born into the jungle,
In the rivers and the trees,
But man the destroyer came for them,
And hunted them mercilessly,
Now all that's left of these animals,
Are handbags, hats and belts,
To fuel a fashion industry,
Where compassion is never felt.

They were born upon the frozen wastes,
Surrounded by arctic seas,
There was no place for them to hide,
No undergrowth or trees,
The destroyer came to kill them,
With batons and sharp knives,
Now all that's left of the white seal pups,
Are fur coats for the rich men's wive's.

The wild animals that used to roam,
The jungles and arctic wastes,
The mighty plains of Africa,
The rivers and the lakes,
All gone now, destroyed my man,
Now they only survive in dreams,
And in repeats of nature programs,
And old wildlife magazines.

Hunted to extinction,
Alas they are no more,
And our children may ask the question,
What the hell did we do that for,
Were we so blind as not to see,
What we would leave behind?
A world devoid of beauty,
The legacy of mankind.

Maybe

Maybe there is heaven,
Maybe there is hell,
Maybe there is magic,
In the wishing well,
Maybe there's an afterlife,
When our time is done,
Maybe fairies dance and sing,
In the early morning sun.

Maybe there are angels,
With wings and halos bright,
Maybe there are demons,
That stalk us in the night,
Maybe there will be world peace,
Hatred in the past,
Maybe the non-believers,
Will see the light at last.

Maybe God is watching,
Wondering what he's done
Maybe he is thinking,
Where did I go wrong?
Maybe man won't kill the Earth,
But allow it to revive
Maybe that is just a dream,
And man may not survive.

Meaning of Christmas?

Christmas time is here again,
And another spending spree,
We'll commit another deadly sin,
One of gluttony,
Trollies piled high with food,
All for just one day,
Just a few slices on the plate,
And the rest is thrown away.

Christmas time is here again,
Increase the debt once more,
On gifts we can't afford to buy,
Is this what Christmas is for?
To purchase the latest gadgets,
The things we can't do without,
Then work all year to pay it off,
Saying that's what it's all about!

Christmas time is here again,
Hitting credit cards to excess,
The money lenders rub their hands,
As you head to a financial mess,
Buying food and presents,
That we don't really need,
Just to satisfy two more sins,
Envy and pure greed.

It seems to me that we've lost sight,
Of what Christmas is really for,
The commercial sector will jump for joy,
As you walk into their store,
So wrap your presents, eat your food,
Celebrate this time of dreams,
Then ask yourself the question,
Is this what Christmas means?

My Oasis

Fairies in the flower beds,
Pixies in the trees,
Goblins share a home with elves,
In a pile of leaves,
They make my garden special,
They talk and play all day,
But when someone comes along,
They run and hide away.

Dragons in the living room,
Warlocks in the hall,
Witches making special brews,
Protecting all my walls,
We all live together,
In perfect harmony,
I'm glad no one can enter,
My world of fantasy.

You may think that I'm quite mad,
Perhaps I am insane,
But there's a very different world,
Beyond my window pane,
A world where no one gives a damn,
A world that doesn't care,
A world that kills for killings sake,
To get to who knows where.

A world that has no pity,
A cold world that is lost,
A world of hateful vengeance,
And hang the human cost,
A world that has no empathy,
With any living thing,
A world that fights the battle,
Where no one really wins.

So I'm quite happy in my world,
My world of make believe,
My oasis in the chaos,
No one can take from me,
And if that makes me different,
From the accepted social norm,
Then walk on by and let me live,
In my world that's calm and warm.

My Pledge

Every minute of every hour,
The wheel of life revolves,
And the mighty God and Goddess,
Has joined our mortal souls,
The ancient ones are with us,
Upon this special day,
The Green Man shall be the witness,
To the words that I now say.

I give you all I have to give,
And all I have is love,
I'll never give you cause to grieve,
While there are stars above,
While there is earth beneath my toes,
And water to cool my skin,
While air surrounds my weary bones,
And the fire burns within.

I'll be beside you all the way,
As we tread the path of life,
That twists and turns each passing day,
In darkness and in light,
So take my hand and walk with me,
Throughout the coming years,
And let the spirits celebrate,
And be forever near.

I pledge to you undying love,
I pledge to you my world,
I'll give to you all that I own,
As the book of life unfolds,
And when at last I must return,
To the Earth from whence I came,
The pledge I give to you this day,
Will forever remain un-changed.

Never Again

Never again will I fall in love,
No more will my heart break,
Never again will I give my all,
For someone else to take,
Now I shall live my life alone,
I'll build my fortress high,
Never again will I lay awake,
No more will these eyes cry.

Never again will I fall in love,
No more shall I feel the pain,
Of broken trust and promises,
Or deceitful lies and blame,
So I'll live my life in solitude,
Shun advances if they're made,
And all those that show an interest,
I shall push them far away.

Never again will I fall in love,
I think it's best that way,
For no one can ever hurt me,
Or take my dreams away,
I'll become a solitary island,
A rock in life's open sea,
Yes I have had my fill of love,
And love's had its fill of me.

Nostalgic Fashion

Teddy Boys from London Town,
Greasers from the States,
In leather jackets and denim jeans,
The Teds wore crepes and drapes,
The fifties gave us Rock and Roll,
A generation left their mark,
Those fashion conscious trend setters,
Emerging from the dark.

Beehive hair and mini skirts,
Mods and Rockers on the beach,
While psychedelic Hippies chanted,
Songs of love and peace,
The sixties fashion exploded,
And London set the trend,
Music mirrored society,
And strikes never seemed to end.

Mini, Midi and Maxi skirts,
Two Tone suits and floral shirts,
New Romantics, Skinheads, Punks,
Glam rock, Soul and Jazz and Funk,
Tartan scarfs, platform shoes,
Hot pants, flares and satin Loons,
Perms for men and Corkscrew hair,
In the seventies no one really cared,

Puffed up shoulders, with frilly shirts,
Pixie boots and Rah-Rah skirts,
Turned up Levi's Five-O-One's
Eighties fashion so full of fun,
Parachute pants hit the London scene
Baggy clothing with anything,
They really thought they looked so hot,
In the decade fashion really forgot!

Ankle Snappers, studded belts,
Cargo jeans and hipsters,
Shirts that tied up around the waist,
Boob Tubes, chokers and Kickers,
The nineties gave us a hotch-potch,
Of different fashion ideas,
A cacophony of grotesque styles,
Mixed from the previous years.

Now we turn to the naughties,
Von Dutch caps and absurd crop tops,
Dress over jeans and bumsters,
Showing all you've got!
Velour track suits for girls and boys,
Shrugs? What was that about?
Peasant tops and pocketless jeans,
Pointless clothing without a doubt!

So that is my nostalgic look,
At fashion throughout the years,
I'm sure that I have missed some trends,
And you have other ideas,
But however bad we must have looked,
Back in our own hay-day,
I'm sure we thought that we looked great!
No matter what others may say.

Not A Tree Hugger

No we are not tree huggers,
Or hippies with tambourines,
Nor do we live in a commune,
And have sunflower seeds for tea,
We won't contribute to the cruelty,
The industry hides so well,
For behind the walls of a slaughterhouse,
Are scenes straight out of hell.

Cattle, sheep, pigs and lambs,
An infant calf for veal,
Screams of fear and blood soaked floors,
So you can have a meal,
The milk you're drinking from the cow,
Is so very full of fat,
But you won't give that a seconds thought,
'Till you have a heart attack!

No we are not tree huggers,
Just ordinary folk,
Who choose to live a cruel free life,
Would you say that that's a joke?
We know that there's an alternative,
To steak and chicken wings,
And an animal like you and me,
Are living, breathing things.

No we are not tree huggers,
And you may laugh and you may scoff,
You may think that we are weirdo's,
Because meat for us is off,
But in the final analysis,
When all is said and done,
We are human just like you,
And enjoy a life of fun.

No we are not tree huggers,
And we eat healthily, thank you,
We get the goodness that we need,
Without meat or dairy too,
Nothing has to die for us,
It really is a shame,
That if you opened up your eyes,
Perhaps you'd be the same.

If you had to kill an animal,
Skin it and cut it up,
Would you really be able to do it?
Would you really have the guts?
No, is probably your reply,
Let someone else carry out the deed,
And you won't have to hear the cries,
Or watch the suffering as it bleeds.

No, we are not tree huggers,
We don't shop in the aisles of death,
We won't eat the fat from the fast food stand,
Or wear clothes made from the dead,
We don't use the fancy makeup,
The industry glamorise,
We see no reason to test these things,
In some poor rabbits eyes.

No we are not tree huggers,
Just compassionate human souls,
An end to pain and suffering,
Is ultimately our goal,
We want to save this planet,
For generations yet to come,
So the youngsters of the future,
Can enjoy a safer sun.

No we are not tree huggers,
We just don't think it's right,
That living things must die for us,
So we can feast each night,
We think that every animal,
That shares this world with us,
Has the right to live its life,
Without fear of the human touch.

No we are not tree huggers,
We're not weird and we're not mad,
But the slaughter of defenceless beings,
For profit makes us sad,
If the animals could talk we ask,
Would you still put up a case,
To see the flesh of a sentient being,
Served upon your plate?

Not my dream

I have no need of churches,
Of goddesses or gods,
I have no need of holy books,
Or symbols like the cross,
I have no need of religion,
I don't believe that God exists,
I cannot subscribe to the fantasy,
Brought on by man-made myths.

Yes I am an atheist,
But a humanist to the core,
I don't believe in suffering,
And I don't believe in wars,
We all live upon this earth,
Each creature that lives and breathes,
And each of us should live in peace,
And that is my belief.

So take your book and prayers my friend,
And leave me here in peace,
I hope you have a happy life,
And find the things you seek,
Yes you have a faith my friend,
A crutch upon which you lean,
So who am I to say you're wrong,
But your faith is not my dream.

October Night

There are many things that haunt you,
Many strange events in life,
So much to be afraid of,
On this dark October night,
Screams or footsteps on the floor,
When no one else is there,
And even though the room is warm,
There's a cold chill in the air.

The veil between the two worlds,
Tonight is very thin,
You may lock your doors and windows,
But the spirits can still come in,
Your crucifix and talisman,
Will not protect you then,
And the hellish cries of this passing soul,
Will call out for its friends.

The demon will knock upon your door,
Scratch at the window pane,
Appear within your living room,
And even know your name,
Move your ornaments from here to there,
Make them fly from left to right,
All these things may happen,
On this dark October night.

A headless corpse may be standing,
At the bottom of your stairs,
A reflection in the mirror,
Its eyes so wide in fear,
Your kitchen could be full of ghosts,
And blood may stain your walls,
You'll feel the icy hand of death,
When the demon come to call.

If you should manage to survive,
Perhaps your friends you'd tell,
How a ghastly demon came to you,
On this night of living hell,
How you cowered beneath your duvet,
And woke to the November light,
Though I am dead, I may come to you,
On this dark October night.

One Chance

We only get one chance at life,
One chance to live and breath,
One chance to walk upon these lands,
Before we have to leave,
But we waste the precious time we have,
Chasing cash and wanting more,
But currency has no value,
When death knocks upon our door.

They only get one chance at life,
One chance to roam this earth,
But this chance is taken from them,
At the moment of their birth,
They're tortured and they're killed and skinned,
So their fur the vain can wear,
Their flesh is cooked and eaten,
By humans who do not care.

We only get one chance at life,
One chance beneath the sun,
But what are we going to leave behind,
For those who've yet to come,
Will we leave a barren, desolate world,
Where animals no longer roam,
And poisoned winds that carry death,
Into each and every home.

We only have one chance at life,
One chance is all we get,
Will we waste this precious time,
In sorrow and regret?
Will we all kneel and pray to a God,
When our blue skies turn to black?
And then we'll find our loving God,
Has closed his eyes and turned his back.

We only get one chance at life,
So let's do the best we can,
Let's not turn this fertile world,
Into a rock of lifeless sand,
Let's leave behind a better place,
Where all can live life's dance
A better world for all that lives,
For we only get one chance.

One Minute

If I could have a minute,
Just one minute more with you,
I'd hold you oh so very tight,
And tell you I love you,
I'd tell you you're my shining star,
And you will always be,
The very best that I have known,
And the very best of me.

If I could have a minute,
Just one minute with you again,
It would be worth the anguish,
The sorrow and the pain,
To feel the love you had for me,
Flow through your fingertips,
To look into your eyes once more,
And see the smile upon your lips.

If I could have a minute,
Just one minute without tears,
I'd tell you what I should have said,
In those living years,
But that can never happen,
And I can never say,
But my darling I think of you,
Every minute of every day.

One Liners?

I think I'll write myself a song,
It don't matter what the lyrics say,
As long as it's got a disco beat,
And the revellers can dance away,
The words don't have to mean anything,
Just a couple of lines will do,
I'll sing them over and over again,
And the music can follow suit.

I think I'll write myself a song,
Call it "Wave your hands in the air",
I'll write "Stamp your feet, turn around,
And together we'll get there",
I'll intersperse it with music,
Sing it again without a care,
They'll play it in the nightclubs,
On the radio and everywhere.

But it will be a rip-off,
Like other one line songs,
Listen to the charts and see,
If I am right or I am wrong,
DJ's will rave about it,
And the kids will learn it too,
There's only a couple of lines to learn,
So it won't be hard to do.

Then I'll buy myself a mansion,
As the royalties flood in,
I'll listen to the radio,
As they play my song again,
It'll take me just five minutes,
To put it on a loop,
Then the engineers can do their thing,
While I pop to the shop.

Songs should have a meaning,
At least I do think so,
It's poetry with music,
But what do I really know,
I do know there are one liners,
Without meaning in the song,
And the artists just don't seem to care,
But maybe, perhaps, I'm wrong.

There's no accounting for taste they say,
And that seems so very true,
I listen to the charts and wonder,
How these "songs" have made it through,
Maybe I'm a dinosaur,
A relic of the yesterday,
Or maybe I'm just out of touch,
With what they're trying to say.

Our First Caravan Trip

We set off on our caravan trip,
Our annual get away,
Me, the wife and our two dogs,
For a summer holiday,
The car was packed and ready to go,
Expectations running high,
We drove away from the city lights,
And excitedly waved goodbye.

The journey to the caravan,
Went so very well,
Not much traffic on the road,
We'd have a great time, we could tell,
We arrived at the caravan storage yard,
Hitched up, there was no going back,
All was going really well,
Then the caravan's tyre was flat!

After much discussion,
And we'd divorced each other twice,
We finally got back on the road,
Harmony restored…., so nice,
But now we were hitting traffic,
Though we really didn't care,
Because we knew good times await,
When finally we get there.

We arrived at our favourite campsite,
No need to erect a tent,
Parked the caravan in the spot,
No wasted time was spent,
As the wife made coffee,
I took the dogs off for a walk,
Got back to a brew, all smiles now,
And we sat and drank and talked.

Day two we went exploring,
Through the forest among the trees,
Charlie and Rosie, our two dogs,
Ran and sniffed quite happily,
The only people on the Earth,
The wife and I strolled hand in hand,
Taking in the sights and smells,
Back to nature and feeling grand.

Day three we went to Lymington,
A pretty coastal town,
Just to get some bits and bobs,
And have a look around,
But the day was really very hot,
And the dogs were suffering,
So the dogs and I found a shady spot,
While the wife done her shopping.

Back to the sanctuary of the caravan,
We sat and had a brew,
Then went into the forest,
With a picnic just for two,
We took something for the dogs of course,
Well, we couldn't leave them out,
And we sat among the ferns and gorse,
As the dogs went on 'sniff about'.

That night we had a thunderstorm,
The rain came crashing down,
But we were cosy, warm and dry,
And we listened to the sound,
The caravan it had no leaks,
No draughts and solid sides,
And we remembered then our tenting days,
When in our sleeping bags we'd hide.

The next few days were much the same,
Blue skies and pleasantly mild,
We took more walks along forest paths,
More time spent in the wild,
We made the most of every day,
In the place that we both adore,
Far away from the bustling streets,
And the grind of the daily chore.

It seemed the day we had to leave,
Had come around too soon,
No more walks along shady tracks,
No more chats under a silver moon,
We packed away our tranquil life,
With sadness in our hearts,
We'd like to stay forever here,
But now we must depart.

We'd woken up each morning,
To skies so clear and blue,
To songs of birds high in the trees,
And squirrels chattering too,
But now there is just silence,
It's as if they seemed to say,
Thank you for your company,
We're sad you're on your way.

The journey home was somber,
Hardly a word was said,
We were lost in the sea of memories,
That floated in our heads,
Even the dogs were quiet,
I wondered if they were sad,
To leave the smells of the forest,
And the wonderful time they'd had.

Now we're back in our house of brick,
Though the car is not too good,
There seems to be a problem,
Somewhere under the hood,
The mechanic said it's time it went,
To that motorway in the sky,
But it's hard to leave a faithful friend,
It's hard to say goodbye.

Our holiday now a memory,
There'll be other times no doubt,
More walks in the forest of our dreams,
And the dogs can run about,
We'll get another car for sure,
And again we'll go away,
But for now we'll have to go to work,
And save for those special days.

Pagan Anniversary

The Green Man was our witness,
The spirits were our guide,
The Lord and Lady looked at us,
From their castles in the sky,
They gave to us their blessings,
As we spoke the sacred vows,
And stood within our circle,
Dressed in our Pagan gowns.

The wheel has turned full cycle,
And brought us to this day,
The day that we professed our love,
In the traditional Pagan way,
The day I gave myself to you,
And you, yourself, to me,
So I say with all my love,
Happy anniversary.

Persephone

When Persephone returns to Hades court,
The flowers will wither and die,
The once green leaves will turn to brown,
And fall as she passes by,
The wind will moan throughout the hills,
The heavens will cry its tears,
And the icy breath of the winter chill,
Will return once more this year.

When Persephone returns to the underworld,
The skies above turn black,
Angry that she has left us,
They'll mourn ''till she comes back,
Snow and ice will rule the land,
The animals will shelter and hide,
They'll not return to walk the earth,
Till again she passes by.

When Persephone sits at Hades side,
Winter once more will rule,
Its icy cloak will bring misery,
To the likes of me and you,
But those that can survive this time,
Will have a treat in store,
For when she returns from Hades Court,
Summer will come once more.

Plastic Lives

Plastic cups, plastic plates,
Plastic knives and forks,
Plastic on the table,
Holding pepper, salt and sauce,
Plastic in the cupboards,
Plastic in the bin,
Plastic going to landfill,
Plastic, a man made sin.

Plastic in the rivers,
Plastic on the beach,
Plastic in the oceans,
Destroying coral reefs,
Plastic eaten by the fish,
Will end up on our plates,
Plastic all around us,
We've made a big mistake.

Plastic bottles, plastic crates,
Where will it all end,
Plastic the great invention,
We thought it was our friend,
Plastic packets on plastic shelves,
Carried home in plastic bags,
And it all ends up in a plastic bin,
It really is quite sad.

We've come to rely on plastic,
You'll see it everywhere,
We'll use it once then throw it out,
And no one seems to care,
It's not the friend we thought it was,
It ruins the environment,
And the only people that can make a change,
Are each nation's governments.

Look around your little home,
You'll see plastic everywhere,
From the cupboards to the TV,
And the bags under the stairs,
In the buses, cars and lorries,
In the garden, in the street,
And some of us are even wearing,
Plastic on our feet!

Surely there's a better way,
A way that does not destroy,
A product we can recycle,
Not pollute this world of joy,
What did we do before plastic,
We still managed to survive,
So do we need our plastic cups,
Plastic plates, and plastic lives.

Pussycats

Dogs in the market square, chasing pussycats,
Listening to the radio,
The old songs take me back,
Back to apple scrumping days,
Playing football in the park,
Back to playing Postman's Knock,
And kiss chase in the dark.

Long and lazy summer days, pussycats on the beach,
Sitting in the sunshine,
Reminds me of the heat,
The heat of youthful loving,
In those days so long ago,
When I was just a puppy,
And pussycats weren't for show.

Now I'm just a grey old dog,
And pussycats saunter by,
In skin tight jeans or mini skirts,
They still catch this old dogs eye,
But my days of chasing pussycats,
Alas have long since passed,
And now I watch the younger pups,
Chase the pussycats in the dark.

Save For The Rainy Days

Save your pennies for a rainy day,
My father once told me,
And I guess I should've listened,
But I was young and fancy free,
My first wage packet in my hand,
Trendy clothes I now could buy,
And the city lights were calling me,
To have a fun filled night.

Put some cash aside, he said,
You'll need it one dark day,
You have to work so hard in life,
Don't fritter it all away,
But he really should've saved his breath,
I didn't listen to a single word,
Those words return to haunt me,
As I walk in a debtors world.

So I went out on the town most nights,
And I had a real good time,
I went abroad on holidays,
A package deal was fine,
I loved and partied all night long,
As only the young can do,
And I couldn't see any rainy days,
For my skies were bright and blue.

But those rainy days were looming,
And of course I couldn't see,
That holidays and fun filled nights,
Would soon be memories,
But I had the comfort of a credit card,
And from the bank a loan or two,
I thought my weekly my wage packet,
Would be enough to see me through.

But the credit card kept mounting up,
I found the loans hard to repay,
The money lenders closed their doors,
So these were the rainy days,
I should've saved those pennies,
Back then when I was young,
I should've listened to my wise old dad,
Instead wasting them on frivolous fun.

Now the credit card company owns my soul,
And what's left the bank will take,
I thought that I could handle things,
And that was a big mistake,
Now I go to work to pay the bills,
In a company that doesn't care,
But they pay me for the job I do,
So I guess, at least, they're fair.

Now I live in a run-down basement flat,
My partner and the kids long gone,
Three more years to repay the debts,
As long as nothing else goes wrong,
Maybe then I'll get my life on track,
And those pennies I'll put away,
At last I'll listen to my father's words,
And save for the rainy days.

Good times are like seconds,
How quickly they fly past,
Although I know the memories,
Throughout my life will last,
But memories don't pay the bills,
When blue skies turn to grey,
Take my advice and save your pennies,
For those far off rainy days.

Shades Of Blue

When I looked into those eyes,
I thought I'd found the one,
I thought I'd found my midnight star,
My early morning sun,
I thought that I had found a dream,
Someone I could cling to,
But the colours the rainbow,
Turned to different shades of blue.

When I was just a teenager,
I thought that life was fun,
I thought that love was just a game,
To walk to but run from,
I thought that there was so much time,
I guess I never knew,
That the colours of the rainbow,
Would turn to different shades of blue.

As I grew much older,
I should've took things seriously,
My friends all said that if I didn't,
I'll just end up so lonely,
I guess I should have listened,
For their words have all come true,
Because the colours of the rainbow,
Turned to different shades of blue.

Now I look upon a photograph,
That face with eyes so bright,
As the shadows creep across my walls,
In the moonbeams silver light,
And memories come back to me,
Of friends that I once knew,
And the colours of my rainbow,
Have turned to shades of blue.

Now I'm lying in my bed,
So cold and so alone,
A priest is murmuring something,
In melodic, dulcet tones,
Is it my soul he's praying for?
As I stare into my doom,
Where the colours of the rainbow,
No longer turn to shades of blue.

If there's one thing that I could say,
Before this world I leave,
Live your days in happiness,
And in your dreams believe,
For the years will pass so quickly,
So this I say to you,
Don't let your rainbows colours,
Turn to different shades of blue.

Soldiers Of The Queen

We were boys when we volunteered,
To serve before the Crown,
We took the oath, our country's coin,
Left the streets of our home towns,
Strangers to each-other, how little we knew then,
That this rag-tag band of innocents,
Would soon be fighting men.

At the training camp we assembled,
These long haired Jack The Lads,
Dressed in the latest fashion,
Our colourful glad rags,
The instructors looked and smiled,
Like us, they once had been,
Now they were trained fighting men,
And soldiers of the Queen.

With subtlety they broke us down,
We didn't see the change,
Strangers became like brothers,
Our lives they rearranged,
From the scruffy chicks that came to them,
The eagle soon would fly,
Disciplined, smart, no longer boys,
But men who were prepared to die.

Basic training over,
We went our separate ways,
Off to our different battalions,
New friendships to be made,
We learned the art of field craft,
And how to stay unseen,
They taught us what it really took,
To be soldiers of the Queen.

We fought together on war torn streets,
And all around the globe,
We followed without question,
And brought our comrades home,
But now the years have passed us by,
New faces fill the ranks,
With pride and honour, they take our place,
And our eternal thanks.

Tactically, the old guard,
Retreats to history,
The bugler sounds the Last Post
As we pass from memory,
But we marched behind The Colours,
Proud that we had been,
A service to our country,
And Soldiers Of The Queen.

Soldiers Retreat

Together they marched into battle,
Together they drank in the Mess,
Together they stood before the flag,
The elite, the very best,
One by one they marched into history,
Good friends who did their time,
But those old soldiers have never died,
They've just retreated behind the line.

Together they fought for freedom,
Together they travelled the globe,
Together they trained in the jungle,
Together they trained in the snow,
Forever these brothers, side by side,
March on although the years unwind,
But those old soldiers will never die,
They'll just retreat behind the line.

So for those who will walk in their footsteps,
For those who will follow the flag,
For those who swell the depleted ranks,
Be proud of the times you'll have,
And like those that marched before you,
No better comrades will you find,
And like those old soldiers you'll never die,
You'll just retreat behind the line.

Some People

Some people are born to be wealthy,
Some people are born to be great,
Some people are born with the Midas touch,
Silver spoons and gold rimmed plates,
Some people are born to be leaders,
Some people are born to follow,
Some people are born to live their lives,
In the shadow of grief and sorrow.

Some people are born to be happy,
Some people are born to be sad,
Some people are born to genius,
Some people are born to go mad,
Some people are born to an easy life,
Some people are born to despair,
Some people are born to be compassionate,
Some people are born not to care.

Some people are born with hate in their heart,
Some people are born to love,
Some people are born to a monastic life,
Forever to search for their god,
Some people are born to be liars and cheats,
Some people are born to be true,
And I have been born with one purpose in life,
That purpose is to love only you.

Special Gift

Last Christmas I made a little wish,
Never thought it would come true,
But Santa Clause must've taken note,
'Cos what he bought to me was you,
So I'll hold you in my arms so tight,
And never let you go,
And look into your eyes so bright,
And say I love you so.

We'll have our ups and downs I'm sure,
As the years go tumbling by,
We'll say some things that we won't mean,
And make each other cry,
But then we'll hold each other close,
And together we will grow,
And every day I'll tell you that,
I really love you so.

You weren't wrapped up in tinsel,
With a card and words so fine,
You weren't encased inside a box,
With ribbon and some twine,
You weren't a Christmas bauble,
Hanging from the tree,
But you were the very best of gifts,
That anyone gave to me.

I'm not quite sure what dad will say,
When he sees me holding you,
I'm not quite sure how he'll react,
When I say you're wonderful,
But there's one thing I can be sure,
I'll love you like no other,
And I will always be with you,
Because I love my baby brother!

Spirit Of The Night

Tomorrow your dreams may find their wings,
And maybe they will take flight,
But for now just drift away,
With the spirit of the night,
Lay within its soft warm arms,
Let its tender kiss caress,
And in the light of a brand new day,
You will wake with hopes refreshed.

The spirit of the night may take you,
On a journey to another world,
A place so weird and wonderful,
Where images will unfurl,
A place where nought can harm you,
And colours do not exist,
As you lay in peaceful slumber,
Within the spirit's warm caress.

The spirit of the night removes,
Your stresses and your strains,
And you will wake to the morning light,
To face your world again,
And when your day is over,
When the moon and stars shine bright,
Once again you'll feel the gentle kiss,
Of the spirit of the night.

Stonehenge

Obscured by the mist of history,
In the shadows of the past,
There lays a tale of wizardry,
And a magic, that today, still lasts,
Is it true, or is it false,
I really cannot say,
For the swirling clouds of time adds words,
And also, takes them, away.

Around the fires on darkened nights,
When the icy wind blew cold,
Children huddled in the flickering light,
To hear a story be retold,
And they in turn passed the story on,
When they were fully grown,
An event that happened in days long gone,
Embellished with bits of their own.

A group of Druids, the story goes,
Gathered one summers night,
Adorned they were in darkened robes,
And a fire they did light,
They all then formed a circle,
And looked toward the sky,
They called to the mighty oracle,
To come and be their guide.

The high priest known as Raven Claw,
Performed the sacred rite,
And as he spoke the wind did cease,
And flames leapt in the night,
A silver chariot seemed to come,
From the moon so full and clear,
As a dragon leapt from the blazing fire,
And its roar they all did hear.

Upon the chariot in a glittering robe,
And a spear forged from the stars,
The moon goddess Arrianhrod stood,
Defiance in her heart,
The dragon she vowed would never take,
The children from her lover's side,
Those that worshipped the sun god,
Would forever stay alive.

She thrust her glittering star forged spear,
Towards the dragons open mouth,
The dragon leapt from the burning flames,
And the Druids had no doubt,
That tonight on the eve of the solstice,
The devil would ride the plain,
And the children of the sun god,
Would never see light again.

A mighty battle then ensued,
Which lasted half the night,
The goddess and the dragon fought,
A ferocious deadly fight,
The Druids stood in their circle,
And chanted in magical tones,
Arrianhrod touched every one of them,
And turned each one to stone.

Each one that is except Raven Claw,
Who took a mighty leap,
Into the burning fire,
As the dragon turned to retreat,
She instantly turned him to stone,
And sealed the dragons escape,
Now the sacrificial altar,
He saved the world from a terrible fate.

The dragon let out an angry roar,
And flames from his mouth did spring,
But the goddess refreshed was far too quick,
And lunged once more at him,
Her spear thrust deep into the dragon's heart,
An explosion split the night,
Then everything went quiet and still,
The goddess had won the fight.

She looked around at the pillars of stone,
Where the Druids once had stood,
And cast a spell so they would remain,
The guardians of the brotherhood,
Seventy Five Druids stood that night,
And there you can see them still,
Standing tall those Sarsen stones,
There on Salisbury Hill.

This story was retold to me,
One winter solstice night,
You may choose not to believe it,
That is, of course, your right,
But before you dismiss this ancient tale,
Ask yourself the question why,
Why Druids gather at the Sarsen Stones,
Upon the Solstice nights.

Sweetly Dream

Lay your head upon the pillow,
Close your eyes and sweetly dream,
Of a wonderful, magical fairyland,
That only you can see,
Where elves and pixies play all day,
Beneath a sparkling sky,
And chocolate covered mountains sing,
Sweet soothing lullabies.

Lay your head upon the pillow,
Close your eyes and drift away,
The fairies will be waiting there,
For you to come and play,
See them in their castles,
That float upon sunbeams,
Lay your head upon the pillow,
Close your eyes and sweetly dream.

And sweetly dream,
Of lollipops and candy covered clouds,
Sweetly dream,
Of fairy dust that spins you round and round,
Sweetly dream,
Of golden fields beneath a blazing sun,
Sweetly dream,
The night away until the morning comes.

Lay your head upon the pillow,
Close your eyes and sweetly dream,
For the rivers of your life will,
Quickly pass you by unseen,
And one day you will wake to find,
That you are fully grown,
And you will whisper words of love,
To children of your own.

Lay your head upon the pillow,
Sweetly dream while you still can,
And one day you will find my love,
That you will understand,
That years are just like petals,
Drifting lost upon life's sea,
Lay your head upon the pillow,
Close your eyes and sweetly dream.

So sweetly dream,
Of lollipops and candy covered clouds,
Sweetly dream,
Of fairy dust that spins you round and round,
Sweetly dream,
Of golden fields beneath a blazing sun,
Sweetly dream,
The night away until the morning comes.

Take a Look (around you)

Take a look around you,
See the beauty of this world,
The sunrise and the sunset,
The baby boys and girls,
They will learn and see much more,
Much more than you and I,
Their future we are making,
Their hopes beyond the sky.

Take a look around you,
See Mother Nature at her best,
The lush green fields and valleys,
The magnificent wilderness,
The bright blue seas and oceans,
The silver rivers and the streams,
The wildlife on the river banks,
In peaceful harmony.

Take a look around you,
At the stunning scenery,
The spectacle of electric storms,
Put on a show for free,
The angry skies may cry it's tears,
The wind may howl all day,
And that is also beautiful,
For that is nature's way.

Take a look around you,
See the joy that love can bring,
The blushing bride, the bashful groom,
Exchanging wedding rings,
They've just begun a journey,
And those memories they'll hold,
They'll begin a new adventure,
As the wheel of life revolves.

Take a look around you,
At the glory of the night,
The stars that cloak the midnight sky,
As the silver moon shines bright,
And we are on this tiny world,
Within a giant galaxy,
And the beauty of the human race,
Lay in the hearts of you and me.

But take a look around you,
You'll see things are not quite right,
Maybe you'll wonder what the day may bring,
With the early morning light,
But only we can make a change,
In the little things we do,
For the beauty of the world is there,
Just waiting for me and you.

For we're the guardians of this Earth,
This oasis in a sea of stars,
And we take it all for granted,
In the belief that it is ours,
But we of course are not alone
There are creatures large and small,
And it is them we must protect,
Or there'll be no beauty at all.

So take a look around you,
See what we have done,
The destruction of the forests,
And wildlife on the run,
Our future generations,
Won't see what we now see,
If we continue to destroy those things,
That bring us such beauty.

Terror

Terror on the subway,
Wrapped inside a bag,
Death behind the steering wheel,
When the mind goes mad,
Gunshots in the dancehall,
Mayhem on the streets,
By fools that bought a vision,
From a seller they'll never meet.

The twisted ideology,
Behind a smile that's thin,
The mask of respectability,
Hides the evil deep within,
Contempt for what does not conform,
To the way they see the world,
Death to those who don't comply,
Put them to the sword.

Hatred dripped into the hearts,
Of those so easily led,
A vision of the glory,
They'll find when they are dead,
But isn't it strange the preachers,
Are still alive and well,
Do they not want the glory,
That they're so keen to sell?

I've never met somebody,
Who's come back from the dead,
And told us that sweet paradise,
Is the thing that lays ahead,
We only have the words of those,
That wrote so long ago,
But they believed the Earth was flat,
So what really did they know?

If we could only open our eyes,
Maybe perhaps we'd see,
That paradise is right in front of us,
In the flowers and the trees,
In the animals of the forest,
In the sun that roams the sky,
In the natural wonders of the world,
That is there for you and I.

It really is a pity,
That this third rock from the sun,
This oasis in the galaxy,
That we all live upon,
Is filled with those intent on death,
It's for God we hear them say,
So they bring their mayhem to our streets,
And their terror to our subways.

The Cold And Icy Sea

Snow was falling gently,
Upon the cold and icy sea,
Surrounding pretty mermaids,
As happy as can be,
Frosty waves were lapping,
On the cold and sandy shore,
Carrying frosty sparkling shells,
To the mermaids watery door.

The mermaids find these pretty shells,
And take them back to shore,
To make the sparkling necklaces,
That they all adore,
Swimming through the icy sea,
To their chilly frosty doors,
Around them hang their necklaces,
To have forevermore.

Evelyn Clifton-Bowley Aged 8

The Final Question

Will the seas become devoid of life,
And will the brotherhood of man,
Sit upon the darkened shores,
Of a lifeless desert land,
Will he look upon the blackened seas,
And cry one final tear,
For all the progress he has made,
Has only brought him here.

Will he try to change his attitude,
In an effort to atone,
Will he look toward the heavens,
To find he's all alone,
Then will he look upon the Earth,
To see a scorched landscape,
And I wonder if he'll realise,
That change has come too late.

And will the grass beneath his feet,
Turn to dust as he picks his way,
Through the derelict houses and rubbled streets,
Where children used to play,
The advances that he thought he'd made,
Now shadows in his mind,
For his greed has only led him ever closer to the grave.

Will he look upon the barren streams,
And remember when life was good,
Look out upon the dusty plains,
Where forests once proudly stood,
Will he seek in vain the animals,
That used to roam the land,
To find that they are all extinct,
Wiped out by the greed of man.

Then will he sit on a hill of sighs,
Like a king upon his throne,
The master of his own demise,
And survey all that he owns,
Will his children then look up at him,
And will he see their moistened eyes,
Will he sit in silence as they ask,
The final question.......Why?

The Girl from across the pond

She was born and raised in Los Angeles,
California in the U.S.A
Like all little girls, perhaps she dreamt,
Of marrying a prince one day,
But the Americans don't have a monarchy,
Unlike Britain where it is strong,
And one day this girl from the sunshine state,
Will stretch her hand across the pond.

He was born into British royalty,
And his father will wear the crown,
His older brother will wear it too,
When his turn comes around,
The young prince will be by his brother's side,
As he has his whole life long,
But no one knew that on his arm,
Would be the girl from across the pond.

An unforeseen, unlikely alliance,
But love has no boundaries,
A British prince, an American actress,
Different cultures that share a dream,
The dream of a lifelong partnership,
Of love that will grow so strong,
A blind date that will put this British prince,
With the girl from across the pond.

The wedding day soon came around,
And the public were invited to see,
As the British and the Americans,
Joined in the pomp and pageantry,
I'm sure if his mother was looking down,
She'd be smiling full of pride,
To see her son with the one he loves,
Her young man with his beautiful bride.

The ceremony may be over,
But for them their lives now start,
The paparazzi recording their every move,
To feed a public's hungry heart,
We wish them luck and happiness,
And we hope their lives are long,
A fairy tale that has come true,
For the girl from across the pond.

The Good Old Days

I was sitting down in my favourite chair,
Blankly staring into space,
When I started thinking of the good old days,
And how much things have changed,
Some perhaps for the better,
Some perhaps for the worst,
And some things haven't changed at all,
Untouched by technologies curse.

When I was a youngster,
A tablet was just a pill,
A telephone was in a telephone box,
And shops used an old fashioned till,
I-pads were not heard of,
Computers were a sci-fi dream,
And if we needed to look things up,
We went to the library.

We called at our friend's houses,
Or we met them in the park,
We ran around like lunatics,
And went home when it got dark,
We drank from the same water bottle,
Climbed trees and had great fun,
And we ate our dinner as a family,
Takeaways had not yet come.

We didn't have the mobile phone,
Or the exclusion a games console brings,
We didn't have social media,
The Internet or technical things,
No cable and no DVD,
No recording facilities,
So we played a game or read a book,
Those were happy days for me.

Now people walk around all day,
Eyes glued to a mobile phone,
Kids do not go out and play,
But stay in their rooms alone,
They meet their friends on Facebook,
And they play their X-Box games,
They eat fatty fast-food takeaways,
Put on weight and who's to blame!

We used our imagination,
In those times of yesterday,
The PC brigade was unheard of,
And we went to a park to play,
Now we face an uphill struggle,
As technology marches on,
And the good old days are history,
The fun days have all gone.

I think that we were greener then,
We didn't throw much away,
Repairing things wherever we could,
In those misty far off days,
Now if something's got a hole in it,
We toss it in the bin,
Go to the shop with our credit card,
And buy the thing again!

Now plastic clogs up the oceans,
There's rubbish in the streets,
Landfills are overflowing,
People sleeping on the streets,
Obesity is on the rise,
Health and safety has gone mad,
Please take me back to the good old days,
The best days I've ever had!

The Old Man Beneath The Tree

An old man sat beneath a wizened tree,
And looked back upon his life,
He thought of all the things he did,
Wondered if they were wrong or right,
The thoughts echoed through his old grey skull,
As the sun beamed on his face,
He closed his eyes and reclined his head,
And the memories began to race.

Images like a picture show,
Flashed on a screen behind his eyes,
A young boy now playing on the beach,
Sand in his ice cream surprise,
Mum and dad were laughing,
As he splashed with them in the sea,
And dad carried home this tired young boy,
Who was too tired to eat his tea.

Now he was a little older,
Playing games and having fun,
Climbing trees and scrumping,
With a group of his childhood chums,
Walking to school in the pouring rain,
Heavy satchel with books on his back,
Messing about in the classroom,
Testing teachers till their patience snapped.

Images now of a fine young man,
Two Tone suit and well groomed hair,
Buttoned down shirt a nice thin tie,
He strides with a certain flair,
Patent leather shoes complete the look,
And he hopes to catch the eye,
Of a pretty young girl in a floral dress,
As he casually saunters by.

The years cascade like a waterfall,
Now with children of his own,
And the pretty young girl in the floral dress,
Has made a home from home,
Hand in hand through the forest trees,
The children play by a silver stream,
And a picnic by the river bank,
Together they plan and dream.

The line between joy and tragedy,
Is very thin indeed,
Together they saw their children wed,
Then his wife was called to leave,
A silver tear rolled down his cheek,
And he wiped the dampness away,
Then he rubbed his hands like he rubbed the dirt,
When he walked away from the grave.

Now all alone with his memories,
A smile forms on his lips,
He remembers the pretty girl he loved,
And he feels the warm breeze kiss,
If you're wondering who the old man was,
Who sat beneath this wizened tree,
Well my friend I thought you would know,
That the grey old man was me!

The Story of Naradine

As a child, Naradine played and ran,
Through the purple canyons of Burgestan,
Those craggy rocks she learnt so well,
And the creatures that within did dwell,
She often sat with a wise old man,
On the hill that looked across the sand,
He taught her the old and magical ways,
That would serve her well in the coming days.

She'd talk with him for hours there,
This wise old man with long white hair,
His skin would turn from bronze to grey,
Depending on the time of day,
The old man took her into the caves,
Where crystals glowed and seemed to change,
And a river flowed but wasn't there,
Where unseen hands tugged at her hair.

He taught her how to summon demons,
And read the minds of men,
He taught her to summon up the wind,
That blew through Burgestan,
He taught her of the flowers,
The animals and herbs,
And how to change the shape of things,
To appear that they weren't there.

He taught her how to move,
Any object with her mind,
And disappear and reappear,
Anywhere at anytime,
He taught her how to glide unseen,
Upon the desert sand,
And how to caste the mirror spell,
And defend Her Burgestan.

One might think that Naradine,
Had no time to play,
Her young mind learning all it could,
Every minute of every day,
But play is a kind of learning,
And magic can be fun,
The old man could stop time for a while,
So she could still play and run.

As she grew, her powers increased,
Her thirst for knowledge never ceased,
She learned illusions, chants and spells,
The wise old man had taught her well,
He taught her to summon the Kalina,
To turn the blue skies black,
How to make them save a soul,
Or make them all attack.

She mourned the day the old man died,
And silver teardrops filled her eyes,
She'd sit alone overlooking the sand,
This golden sea of Burgestan.

Her fifteenth birthday came along,
And a mighty army fierce and strong,
Had gathered on the sea of sand,
Preparing to invade young Naradine's land,
She'd heard the stories from men who'd fled,
How this merciless army left only the dead,
How villages, towns and cities fell,
To these marching men that came from hell.

Now Burgestan was in their sights,
Its precious crystals that gleamed at night,
Was highly prized by the evil Lord,
For their power was greater than a thousand swords,
He'd learned that the wise old wizard had died,
And he assumed that no one else alive,
Knew of the power those crystals held,
And he'll mine them all when Burgestan fell.

Naradine watched as ten thousand men,
Prepared to camp on the sand and then,
The old man appeared in the fading light,
A silvery shadow glowing bright,
His words were as soft as a summer breeze,
And Naradine's joy was plain to see,
Her wise old friend she'd known so well,
She heard his voice as the sunlight fell.

Remember the mirror spell my child,
Remember the wind can be calm or wild,
Remember the crystals within the caves lie,
Use them all well, let your enemies die,
Suddenly a flash and without a trace,
The wise old man disappeared in space,
And Naradine woke as if from a dream,
And remembered the teachings, what she'd done and seen.

Two hundred militia stood side by side,
And looked at the army so far and wide,
Ten thousand warriors a few miles away,
Burgestan will fall the following day,
Naradine saw the fear in their eyes,
They couldn't stand against an army so wide,
And Naradine vowed as the stars shone bright,
To use all he'd taught her in those long days and nights.

She rushed to her home in the old market square,
Where the merchants would gather and trade all their wares,
She took the long staff that was once the old man's,
Then gathered the crystals and to the hill ran.

The army had camped, their fires burned bright,
Turning the darkness to flickering light,
Their voices were carried to her on the breeze,
And a blue mist rose from a circle of trees,
She held up the staff and the crystals glowed red,
Like the eyes of a dragon, soulless and dead,
And all the time the blue mist still rose,
'Till Naradine was covered from her head to her toes.

Her voice began low, like rumbling stones,
The staff had turned white, like sun bleached bones,
She chanted the mirror spell, the crystals now shone,
And the blue mist rose higher and then it was gone,
Now she must wait for the new sun to rise,
The soldiers may sleep for tomorrow they'll die,
Naradine would bury them deep in the sand,
Never to set foot in Her Burgestan.

The soldiers struck camp as the new sun did rise,
And they noticed a strange blue cloud fill the skies,
And there on the hill, two hundred did stand,
The only resistance from poor Burgestan,
They picked up their weapons and formed neat smart rows,
And headed for Burgestan, the pace it was slow,
With each step they took, 'neath the strange cloudy skies,
Burgestan's army seemed to double in size.

Naradine stood and watched the army draw near,
She could sense the militia men's hearts and their fear,
Her voice was commanding, bewitching and strong,
And the men stood stock still, as if made of stone,
The army then stopped some distance away,
And the archers came forward, their arrows would lay,
A barrage of death to those on the hill,
But the militia men stood defiant and still.

A thousand arrows were sent to the sky,
Up through the cloud that above now did lie,
Then a thousand more shafts were sent on their way,
Those on the hill will perish this day.

The militia then heard the death screams of men,
As the arrows returned to the earth once again,
But it wasn't the screams of those on the hill,
But from the army below and the arrows came still,
Two thousand arrows returned to the land,
And soldiers were speared and died on the sand,
As a thousand more shafts were despatched to the hill,
Just to return, to maim and to kill.

Naradine stood, her staff she held high,
And the blood red crystals formed dragons eyes,
She uttered a chant and the crystals turned green,
Then dragons appeared where the crystals had been,
She pointed her staff and the dragons took flight,
The sun clouded over, now in the half light,
The dragons ripped through the ranks of her foe,
The militia men watched the horror below.

Soldiers lay bleeding, dying or dead,
A dark mist had formed around Naradin's head,
The evil Lord screamed, had he been deceived?
The old man was dead he was led to believe.
But there on the hill the figure he saw,
As a dragon past by with a deafening roar,
The wizard of Burgestan, shrouded in mist,
His staff was held high in a thin tiny fist.

The dragon assault was brutal and fast,
The soldiers were glad that it didn't last,
Now they assembled, reforming their ranks,
The evil Lord ordered the trolls to the flanks,
Tall as elephants, these mighty trolls are,
Feared by all, no matter how far,
Their shoulders so broad, so thick and so wide,
They cover ten paces in only one stride.

Arms thick as tree trunks, and huge fists like stone,
Their voice deep and booming, a frightening, groan,
They're big and clumsy, and they don't feel much pain,
But the problem with trolls, they have very small brains!
Easily confused, so they must be led,
And they'll be your friend as long as their fed,
Not much can stand in the way of a troll,
A great friend to have but a merciless foe.

The evil Lord stood, the air it was still,
He pointed his sword to those on the hill,
Then in a voice that reached every man,
He cried show no mercy to all Burgestan!

The army as one, began to advance,
And as they did so, the air seemed to dance,
For Naradine chanted and held the staff high,
And a ferocious wind came from the sky,
Trolls now are scared, the wind calls their name,
They believe that the spirits will drive them insane,
They turn from the front and rush to retreat,
Trampling the soldiers under their feet.

Undeterred by the wind, the army advanced,
Horses in front, their riders with lance,
And Burgestan's little army moved to,
But not the two hundred, they could not move,
Closer and closer the armies became,
And Naradine watched, her eyes were aflame,
The two hundred stood with swords in their hand,
They knew they would die for their Burgestan.

From the hilltop they saw the army below,
Wielding their swords to strike and to blow,
They couldn't believe the sight or the sound,
For each time they struck a soldier fell down,
The evil Lord screamed, he could not believe,
His army was now fighting something unseen,
And there on the hilltop he saw the old man,
The lone figure that stood to defend Burgestan.

His spies they had told him the old wizard was dead,
And Burgestan's army was small an ill led,
This city he'd take and then wear the crown,
And proclaim himself king of the lands all around.

In the midst of this battle his own wizard he called,
Now he would see this Burgestan fall,
His wizard was dark with a heart black as coal,
He had no compassion, no pity, no soul,
He conjured up spirits and murmured a spell,
Those on the hill would soon be in hell,
One bony finger pointed the way,
As hundreds of spirits darkened the day.

Toward the hilltop they sped through the air,
The evil Lord laughed, this day would be theirs,
The spirits then disappeared into the mist,
And the evil Lord raised a triumphant fist.

Lightning erupted from the mist on the hill,
Then suddenly the wind became silent and still,
Then with a mighty deafening roar,
The spirits lay scattered like leaves on the floor,
The evil lord's wizard looked on with surprise,
For in front of him stood, with dark angry eyes,
The thousands of souls he had sent to their graves,
Now they'd returned to take his powers away.

Naradine pointed her staff once again,
The evil Lord heard the scream and the pain,
From his wizard in agony there on the ground,
Begging for mercy where none would be found.

The scream was unbearable like thousands in pain,
The evil lord thought it would drive him insane,
Then with a mighty blow of his axe,
Killed his old friend in a frenzied attack,
He stood and he looked but couldn't recall,
The frenzied attack that saw his friend fall,
But the blood on his axe told its own tale,
And then he ex hailed a loud painful wail.

He was looking with sadness at his fallen friend,
Then vowed and declared he'd have his revenge,
But his soldiers had covered not one inch of ground,
And above him he heard a deafening sound.

He looked up and saw the sky turning black,
As a thousand Kalina began to attack,
Wings six feet long with talons like steel,
And a beak that could break the strongest ships keel,
Through the ranks of his soldiers the Kalina did sweep,
Tearing and ripping with talons and beak,
They circled and swooped and attacked once again,
What other horrors upon them would rain?

The soldiers were screaming in fear and in dread,
On the sand were the dying, the wounded and dead,
And there on the hill a dark mist growing higher,
In the centre of which there was lightening and fire,
Ten thousand soldiers had sought to invade,
The city of Burgestan on that fateful day,
The Evil Lord didn't know the one who lived there,
This very young sorceress with long golden hair.

Now his army before him lay dead in the sand,
Those that were left had turned and had ran,
Now the evil Lord stood bewildered, alone,
His dreams and ambitions like the Kalina had flown.

Then all was quiet and eerily still,
He looked and he saw the men on the hill,
And standing in front with her staff in the air,
A pretty young girl with long flowing hair,
Suddenly he was standing there on the hill,
With two hundred men who wanted to kill,
But Naradine's voice commanded they stay,
And they did as she said and then cleared a way.

The evil Lord stayed in Burgestan's jail,
For the rest of his life he moaned and he wailed,
She took his mind with a touch of her hand,
He should never have tried to take her Burgestan.

The cities and towns and little hamlets,
Were free from this tyrant now under arrest,
And everyone heard what happened that day,
When a powerful young sorceress took evil away.

As a child, Cherapon played and he ran,
Through the purple canyons of Burgestan,
The craggy rocks where strange creatures did dwell,
And Naradine taught the young boy so well.

In the centre of Burgestan's old market square,
They built a bronze statue that still remains there,
A statue of Naradine just fifteen years old,
And to all of the visitors, this story is told.

The Story Teller

You can be the story teller,
Just let your mind run wild,
You can be a mighty wizard,
Or whatever you desire,
You can raise an army,
And set the people free,
Or fight a host of dragons,
And be home in time for tea.

You can be the story teller,
Regardless of your age,
You can solve a mystery,
You can be a wise old sage,
You can discover planets,
That have weird fantastic beasts,
Or you can crack a spy ring,
Before your mid-day feast.

You can be the story teller,
Imagination is the key,
You can make it all seem real,
Though it's just fantasy,
Transport us all to another place,
Somewhere no one has seen,
You can make it a nightmare,
Or a wonderful love filled dream.

You can be the story teller,
So tell your tale to me,
Put your thoughts upon the page,
So that I may read,
I'll head to far off places,
Transported by your hand,
Your thoughts are all I really need,
To live in another land.

They Stood before the Colours

They stood before the Colours,
Defenders of the Crown,
Those fresh faced youths,
Those childhood pals,
Who grew up in the same old town,
They heard their country calling,
They saw the marching band,
They enlisted all together,
Waved farewell to their mum and dad.

They stood before the Colours,
Accepted their country's coin,
They marched away with beaming smiles,
Though not much more than boys,
They went looking for adventure,
But all they found was death,
And they cradled their friends,
In blood soaked arms,
As they drew their final breath.

They stood before the Colours,
Proud soldiers everyone,
And a nation paid the price of war,
With the blood of their bravest sons,
Some returned scarred and victorious,
Each with a tale to tell,
How they left the trenches in a foreign field,
And marched straight into hell.

They stood before the Colours,
And over the top they ran,
Obey the order to advance,
Across a muddy no-man's land,
One big push for victory,
Before the rising sun,
Young lives cut short in a bullet storm,
And the sound of rattling guns.

They stood before the Colours,
On land and air and sea,
They stood against the hordes of hell,
And defeated tyranny,
They paid the ultimate sacrifice,
Now in a foreign land,
Are headstones in their thousands,
With the names each young man.

They stood before the Colours,
And boys returned as men,
We can only guess at the horrors they faced,
In the hell holes like Arnhem,
At home the women suffered too,
As Satan's demons struck,
But they kept the home fires burning,
And Satan ran out of luck.

They stood before the Colours,
With smiles they went to war,
Now I look around and ask myself,
What did they do this for?
Because it hasn't changed a single thing,
Man cannot live in peace,
And the evidence is plain to see,
On the bombed out blood soaked streets.

Times Of You And Me

Old songs playing on the radio,
Bring back sweet memories,
Of glorious, wonderful, far off days,
Those times of you and me,
Those moments only we could share,
Those coach trips to the sea,
I close my eyes and dream about,
Those times of you and me.

Images dancing on the TV screen,
Remind me of the past,
Reflecting on plans that we once had,
But our dream just wouldn't last,
Somehow we went our separate ways,
Though why is a mystery,
And I close my eyes and dream about,
Those times of you and me.

People walking hand in hand,
Just like we used to do,
Talking, laughing, having fun,
Lovers forever true,
But somewhere along the road of life,
They set each other free,
Now I close my eyes and dream about,
Those times of you and me.

Now I sit within my little room,
And watch time slip away,
Sunbeams bounce off the photographs,
Those memories of yesterday,
Those precious moments we both shared,
When we were so happy,
And I close my eyes and dream about,
Those times of you and me.

And I wonder where you went to,
What sort of life you've had,
Has it been filled with happiness,
Or has it been lonely and sad,
And do I ever cross your mind,
When the moonbeams kiss the sea,
And do you close your eyes to dream,
Of those times of you and me.

I looked through the misty window,
I sat and watched life pass,
I heard the songs on the radio,
Watched lovers walk in the park,
I saw the silent images,
Dancing on my TV screen,
Now one last time I close my eyes,
On those days of you and me.

When Nature's Cloak Turns White

Winter's cloak lays loosely,
On the branches and the boughs,
Once green fields now white with snow,
No place for sheep and cows,
And icicles like the fairy lights,
That adorn a Christmas tree,
Twinkle in the winter sun,
In the leaves of the evergreens.

Unseen fingers draw icy shapes,
Upon the window panes,
A welcome fire that seems to say,
Come warm yourself by my flames,
Some people walk the frozen streets,
Wrapped up to keep the cold at bay,
And some stay warm and dry at home,
Upon this winter's day.

A frozen pond in the village square,
Thatched roofs now covered with snow,
A picturesque scene like the greeting cards,
That we have come to know,
A robin fluffs its feathers,
And sings a chirpy song,
As a fox trots back to the snowy woods,
Back home to where it belongs.

As the winter sun slowly disappears,
Behind the snowy hills,
So stars appear in the cloudless sky,
And the evening has an extra chill,
The moonbeams shine on the icy ground,
Silver crystals sparkling bright,
And all is quiet in this frozen land,
On this cold, cold winters night.

I've walked in this icy wonderland,
Seen snow covered fields and trees,
Seen the frozen pond in the village square,
And natures majesty,
Now as I step into my little home,
I smile and recall the sight,
Of the beauty that surrounds us,
When nature's cloak turns white

White Witch of the Woods

Walking through the woods one day,
A few years ago, in early May,
The morning sun was shining down,
Forming dappled shadows upon the ground,
I wasn't really thinking much,
Idly reaching out to touch,
A leaf perhaps upon a branch,
Or watch squirrels playfully dance.

No one else was walking there,
I was all alone in the morning air,
Just taking in the scenery,
And the beauty that surrounded me,
The woods were silent, and a gentle breeze,
Not strong enough to stir the leaves,
And oh so softly kissed my cheek,
As the squirrels carried on playing hide'n'seek.

I turned around and suddenly,
A lady was in front of me,
Dressed in white from head to toe,
On her shoulders, a raven and a crow,
How old she was I couldn't tell,
I seemed to be held in a kind of spell,
I couldn't move, I couldn't speak,
The earth itself seemed to grip my feet.

The raven and crow took to flight,
I stood transfixed at this awesome sight,
They began to circle above my head,
And I didn't hear what the lady had said,
Then unseen hands were holding me,
And everything was spinning furiously,
Yet not one single leaf was stirred,
This must be a dream, my brain inferred.

Then she spoke in a gentle voice,
I listened intently, I had no choice,
Her words were soft and very kind,
Which put to rest my frightened mind,
She told the story of this wood,
Her name was Adaryn I understood,
I thought that's Welsh and meaning bird,
I remember thinking that's so absurd.

As she spoke I could plainly see,
Tiny insects within the trees,
Hidden beneath the woody bark,
Living quite happily in the dark,
I saw the liquid pumping through,
The veins of leaves and plant life too,
Pushed from the heart of underground bulbs,
And watched their respective leaves unfold.

She said we look but never see,
The magic and the real beauty,
Although we listen we never hear,
The sounds of nature so very near,
Through various visions I was led,
And all the while above my head,
The raven and crow circled endlessly,
Their beating hearts became clear to me.

At last they returned to the lady in white,
And I saw the woods in a different light,
The lady stood with her raven and crow,
Perched on her shoulders, eyes aglow,
Then they were gone in the blink of an eye,
I looked all around and noticed up high,
A raven and crow flying East to the sun,
I looked for Adaryn, but she too had gone

Now when I walk on this magical path,
I hear Adaryn's voice saying,
"Look with your heart",
I've not seen her since,
But dearly wish that I could,
See once again,
The White Witch of the Woods.

When Santa Clause Got Stuck

One cold and snowy Christmas Eve,
Santa had a mighty shock,
He climbed half way down the chimney,
But the chimney breast was blocked!
He couldn't climb any further down,
Nor could he climb back up,
He was in an awful pickle,
For he was well and truly stuck!

Rudolph and the others,
Were waiting on the roof,
What's keeping him asked Dasher,
And he stamped his muffled hoof,
Prancer looked at dasher,
Smiled and blinked his eyes,
He's probably drinking sherry, he said,
And eating warm mince pies.

Prancer called to Santa,
Come on, don't muck about!
We've still got loads of presents here,
And time is running out,
The children won't get their little gifts,
If you don't hurry up,
Then they heard his muffled cry,
I can't cos I've got stuck!

Santa yelled "I'm really stuck,
I can't move my arms or legs,
And this sack is feeling heavy,
Cos it's resting on my head,
Bring the magic thinning dust,
It's in my big lunch bag"
Donner looked at Blitzen,
Who's carrot he'd just had.

Did your head get a little knock?
Vixen asked and gave a neigh,
I thought by now you might have known,
We're all tied to this sleigh!,
So have you another bright idea,
Or must we spend the night,
Standing on this rooftop,
Till the stars go out of sight!

Maybe we should leave him here,
Go back and get some help,
Rudolph said Comet,
Then shook the bells upon his belt,
They murmured to each-other,
The way that reindeers do,
Then from the chimney they all heard,
A very big aitchoo!

Get the magic thinning dust,
Vixen then chipped in,
The stuff that Bushy Evergreen made,
That'll make him thin,
He's just said that, said Rudolph,
You really must clean your ears,
He said it's in his lunch box,
Which we can't get anywhere near!

Then they heard a voice call out,
From behind the big toy sack,
Well it's not inside his lunch box,
 Wunorse Open-sleigh shouted back,
Then they heard a murmur I forgot to pick it up!
On that cold and snowy Christmas Eve,
When Santa Clause got stuck.

Donner said to Dancer,
We can't hang around all night,
Somehow we've got to get him out,
It'll soon be getting light,
Perhaps we should get back to base,
And bring that thinning dust,
Or Christmas will be ruined,
And there will be a mighty fuss!

The reindeer looked at each other,
Sighed and shook their heads,
Bushy Evergreen will not be pleased,
It took her months to make that stuff,
And what about the toy makers,
You know they'll scream and shout,
We've got to think of another way,
To get old Santa out.

Rudolph looked around and said,
We could do it I suppose,
Deliver all these little gifts,
Then blew his bright red nose,
Don't be daft! Said Dancer,
You know we'll muck it up!
If we tried to get down the chimney,
Then we would all get stuck!.

Would you like me to tell you all,
What's going through my mind?
The devilish little plan I've hatched,
To get us back on time,
A plan to get the big guy out,
And deliver all the toys,
So this disastrous Christmas Eve,
Can end on a note of joy?

The reindeer looked at Rudolph,
And in unison replied,
Go on then red nose what's the plan,
And each of them then sighed,
It's bound to be something stupid,
Comet huffed and puffed,
On that cold and snowy Christmas Eve,
When Santa Clause got stuck.

Rudolf took no notice,
Well I think you'll all agree,
That Blitzen is the fastest here,
With his super lightening speed,
It'll only take him minutes,
To pick up that thinning dust,
He'll be back before we know it,
Then Santa could get unstuck.

Prancer said there's just one flaw,
In that otherwise brilliant plan,
In case you haven't noticed,
Reindeer's don't have hands!
How do you propose that we,
Undo these bob sleigh straps
When none of us can even reach,
An itch upon our backs!

I could undo those harness straps,
Shouted Wunorse Open-sleigh
I am very quick you know,
Then we could be on our way,
And he added, with a grin,
I know where they hide that stuff,
On that cold and snowy Christmas Eve,
When Santa Clause got stuck.

They were back within a jiffy,
Thinning potion safe and sound,
Mrs Clause was not too pleased,
Said Blitzen with a frown,
I think old Santa's in for it,
There's bound to be a ruck,
On that cold and snowy Christmas Eve,
When Santa Clause got stuck.

Rudolf said, well use it quick,
We cannot hang about,
That thinning dust will do the trick,
We need to get old Santa out,
So Santa Clause was rescued,
And Christmas was back on track,
On that cold and snowy Christmas Eve,
When Santa Clause got stuck.

All the presents got delivered,
So no real harm was done,
The reindeer were all tucked up in bed,
Before the rising sun,
Santa said to Mrs Clause,
I guess it was just bad luck,
But none could forget that Christmas Eve,
When Santa Clause got stuck.

Acknowledgements

My thanks go to Mathew and Hayley Clifton-Bowley for allowing me to include the poem 'The Cold and Icy Sea', written by their eight year old daughter Evelyn, in this offering.

I would also like to thank my wife, Julie, for being my sounding board and critic. Without her, some of these may never have made the book in their present form.

www.ingramcontent.com/pod-product-compliance
Lightning Source LLC
Chambersburg PA
CBHW031630210526
45464CB00004B/1836